Geoffrey Grogan was born in Bristol in 1925 and grew up in a nominal Christian environment. At the age of twenty he was converted through contact with vibrant Christians and through reading a book by C.S.Lewis. He studied theology first at Glasgow Bible Training Institute and then at London Bible College, joining the staff of BTI in 1951 until transferring to the staff of LBC in 1965. In 1969, he became principal of BTI where he served until his retirement in 1990. He was awarded a doctorate in 1998 by the Open University Senate for his outstanding contribution to tertiary theological education.

From 1973 he served for twenty-six years as chairman of the Scottish Evangelical Theological Society (originally known as the Scottish Tyndale Fellowship). Among his deepest concerns are world mission, evangelical unity on a firm biblical basis, and effective communication of biblical truth and its application to daily living.

His immense enthusiasm for Biblical Theology inspired the new *Dictionary of Biblical Theology* (IVP 2000) as well as other publications such as a 21st century study on biblical anthropology. His own very extensive writings include *Christ of the Bible and the Church's Faith*, commentaries on Mark's Gospel and 2nd Corinthians (Focus on the Bible series), *Is That Your Voice, Lord?*, *Shaping Tomorrow Starting Today*, *Wrestling with the Big Issues*, as well as innumerable articles in various theological journals and chapters in published collections of learned papers. For the first six years of his retirement, he served as pastor of Kirk O'Shotts Baptist Church. Though now fully retired, he continues to be active in writing and theological research.

There is an urgent need for mainline churches to move from maintenance to mission. Here, in short compass, are the reasons for that transition and why the church needs to act now. These articles should move us to prayerful and thoughtful action.

J. Stafford Carson
Westminster Theological Seminary

Devolution is the in-word politically. Spiritually England and Scotland preach the same gospel and fight similar battles. As one who has ministered on both sides of the border I have found this book compelling, disturbing, and yet hopeful reading.

Philip Hacking

Informative and inspirational. Theological and practical. The value of *Death and Glory* is that it offers a look at mission in Scotland from several different angles, helping us to gain our 360^0 perspective. Scotland cannot rely on its spiritual heritage from the past. I hope this helpfully challenges the church to face the task of the future. It would be a sin if those in other parts of the United Kingdom did not read and benefit from these reflections. There is so much that those south of the border and elsewhere can learn.

Derek Tidball,
Principal,
London Bible College

Death or Glory

Edited by
David Searle

Mentor
Rutherford House

© Rutherford House
ISBN 1 85792 629 3
published in 2001 by
Christian Focus Publications,
Geanies House, Fearn, Ross-shire,
IV20 1TW, Great Britain
and
Rutherford House,
17 Claremont Park, Edinburgh,
EH6 7PJ, Great Britain

Contents

FOREWORD

'You have to recognise realities in order to change them.' These wise words from a top diplomat, Egon Bahr, former political adviser to Willy Brandt, the German Chancellor, carry a challenging resonance for all who are concerned about the mission of the Church in Scotland in a new millennium.

Scotland today is very different from the Scotland of 1846 when, with the significant backing of Thomas Chalmers and his Presbyterian colleagues, the Evangelical Alliance first came into being. While one in seven Scots still attend church on a Sunday, the Christian cause is increasingly marginalised. A recent System 3 poll in *The Herald* showed that 44% believed religion had only 'a minor part' to play in Scottish public life. A further 9% said it 'plays no part at all'. Just 8%, mainly the core committed Christian constituency, felt it played a major part. An editorial concluded in these terms: '...organised religion is losing its place within Scottish society. Our latest survey confirms the suspicion that religion plays little or no part in the life of a majority of Scots. We are therefore living in what must be by any reasonable definition, a secular society. Does this matter?' (*The Herald*, 6 December 1999).

How we as Christians and as churches respond together to this defining moment, and to these twin challenges of declining faith commitment and growing secularisation, will almost certainly shape, under God, the new Scotland in a new millennium.

It was for these compelling reasons, amongst others, that the Scottish Evangelical Theological Society approached the Evangelical Alliance Scotland and invited us jointly to host a special conference for theologians and church leaders on the theme *Death or Glory? The church's mission in Scotland's changing society*. The Conference was to commemorate the 150th Anniversary of the founding of the Evangelical Alliance, and took place in the Faith Mission Bible College in Edinburgh in April 1996. Central to our concerns was the. need to bring together a range of expert contributors to address the whole theme of mission in Scotland today and, in particular, those realities that first require to be recognised before they can ever be changed. What is the cultural backdrop to contemporary Christian mission (chapter 1)? What vital lessons can we learn from the past 150 years of Christian mission (chapters 2 and 3)? How do we best communicate the essence of the gospel in Scotland today (chapter 4)?

Mission in practice then forms the basis of a church and para-church approach in two fascinating case studies (chapters 5 and 6). The book continues with a strong affirmation of the Christian church, biblically defined and practically demonstrated, as God's primary agent in mission (chapter 7). The concluding paper then examines the crucial importance and the practical implications of a biblical vision of revival alongside a radical commitment to mission as offering genuine grounds for optimism as we begin a new millennium.

It was no coincidence that one of the prime movers behind this conference was my friend and colleague Dr Geoffrey Grogan. For many years the highly esteemed Principal of the Bible Training Institute in Glasgow (now the International Christian College), Geoffrey combines the finest qualities of good New Testament scholarship with a passion for evangelism marked by biblical clarity, warm sensitivity and a wholehearted devotion to Christ. So while in one sense this book commemorates 150 years of the Evangelical Alliance, we are only too glad to dedicate these significant contributions on the theme of mission to this 'gentle giant' of the faith, and the countless ordinary Christians who over the past 50 years found, through his words, the living Word and responded to the call of Christ both at home and abroad.

'How is it,' an English Baptist minister commented recently, 'that we have taken the most relevant person for our generation – Jesus Christ – and managed to convince everyone of His irrelevance?' That is the nub of the challenge facing the Christian church here in Scotland today in a society when 90% of our young people have no formal links with the church, and even 70% of our elderly population are non-churchgoers. The task of mission, the truth of the Christian gospel and the type of evangelism we engage in have never been more important or more urgent. What better time to encourage the gift of evangelism throughout the church, to equip ministers and pastors with the training and the tools to do the job and to empower our pew-fillers to be active faith-sharers?

As a strategic contribution to that urgent task, we offer these pages in the firm conviction that if God only needed fewer, better people, rather than more people, to set the Christian gospel rolling 2000 years ago, perhaps he is once again calling his people together in Scotland for such a time as this to do something very similar and equally necessary as we begin a new millennium.

'It was a small group of eleven men whom Jesus commissioned to carry on his work.... In their own nation they were nobodies.... If they had stopped to weigh up the probabilities of succeeding in their mission, even granted their conviction that Jesus was alive and that his Spirit went with them to equip them for their task, their hearts must surely have sunk, so heavily were the odds weighted against them. How could they possibly succeed? And yet they did.' (Michael Green, *Evangelism in the Early Church,* Eerdmans, Grand Rapids, Michigan, 1970, p.13).

Our grateful thanks to all the contributors, and a special thank you to my good friend and colleague, David Searle and the staff at Rutherford House for their excellent work in editing and preparing these scripts for publication.

David J. B. Anderson
General Secretary,
Evangelical Alliance Scotland

FOREWORD

Churches are dying in Scotland in the infancy of the twenty-first century of the Christian era. Most readers of this book are likely to know of a place not too far away where a congregation of Christ's church used to exist not too long ago but exists no more. A few weeks before I wrote this Foreword the Presbytery of Edinburgh of the Church of Scotland decided that a congregation serving a parish with a population fast approaching 10,000 was 'no longer viable ... on its last legs'. The best way forward was to 'draw a line under the existing congregation and start again from scratch'. The debate in the Presbytery was conducted in sober tones, as others were stirred to recognize that their congregations too were dying. Would the same happen to them? Not often, in my experience, is the Christian church able to bear so much reality. It has precious little glory about it.

It is my hope that this collection of papers will help a wide range of people concerned with the health of Christ's church to face its situation realistically in the broader perspectives of historical, cultural and social analysis, as well as more direct prescriptions for mission today. No single blueprint emerges; indeed, significant differences of diagnosis and aspiration are clearly recognizable. But all the contributions are united in a commitment to evangelism as irreducibly central to the mission of the church. One would expect nothing less from a conference sponsored jointly by the Scottish Evangelical Theology Society and the Evangelical Alliance of Scotland, to mark the 150th anniversary of the foundation of the Alliance. Two such 'Evangelical' bodies were bound to promote a sharp focus on the evangel and the inexorable claims its service makes on the imagination and energies of Christian people.

The point should not be taken too easily, for evidence is not lacking that some in the Scottish churches have given up on evangelism. In some quarters Luke 4:16-21 is given explicit

preference over the 'Great Commission' of Matthew 28:18-20.
The most recent report from the Scottish Church Initiative for
Union accepted that 'Christians will differ to the extent to which
they understand the purpose of mission as "winning souls for
Christ" and building up the numerical strength of the Church'.
No wonder congregations die! – or live on as organisations or
communities decreasingly Christian in identity. That way lies a
more comfortable existence in a culture less and less hospitable
to witness to Jesus Christ as the Saviour of the world and the
Lord of lords.

The saving grace of Edinburgh Presbytery's resolution to
bid a dying congregation a sad farewell was its clarity in
determining where would lie 'the responsibility for raising a
new community of God's people in ....'. Readers can supply a
place-name for themselves, in their knowledge of a place bereft
of a local witness to the gospel of Christ. May this book nourish
a like determination to raise new communities of God's people
in an increasingly deChristianized Scotland.

David Wright
Professor of Patristic and Reformation History,
New College, University of Edinburgh

Chapter 1

The Culture of Modern Scotland
As The Context for Christian Mission:
A View From Over the Border

David Smith

What is Scotland?

I. The shaping of Scottish culture

There are a variety of ways in which we can seek to gain an understanding of the culture of a particular nation or people. In relation to modern societies, one source of information is what is called public art: monuments, public buildings, statues.

1. Public art

Monuments

So far as Scotland is concerned the statues erected in Edinburgh tell a very interesting story. The monument which dominates the centre of the city is of course that which houses the statue of Sir Walter Scott. Just beside this there is a statue depicting the great nineteenth-century Christian missionary, David Livingstone. Glasgow also has a statue of Livingstone, and his birthplace at Blantyre has functioned as a Scottish National Memorial since 1925. A few hundred yards from the Livingstone statue in Princes Street we come upon memorials in stone honouring two outstanding Evangelical preachers—Thomas Guthrie and, looking down from George Street, Thomas Chalmers. From this vantage point we can look across to New College on the Mound, knowing that just inside the entrance there is to be found a huge statue of another Protestant preacher, the reformer John Knox. Is there any other city in the world in which public art reflects the impact of evangelical religion on national history and culture in such a remarkable way?

Consider the contrast with London. I am not aware of any monument erected there in public space to honour a missionary or an evangelical preacher. The best known statue in London is that of Lord Nelson and the capital is dotted with the figures of past political and, especially, military heroes. In the last few years the appearance of Whitehall has been changed by the erection of a series of statues and busts commemorating recent military leaders, and the Strand now hosts the controversial statue of 'Bomber' Harris.

It is worth quoting here the reaction of a great English preacher in the nineteenth century to the erection of the statues of military leaders in London. Here is Charles Haddon Spurgeon preaching for the Baptist Missionary Society in 1857: the Gospel, he says, is a message of peace, and when it has the success promised to it in Scripture then 'wars must cease to the ends of the earth'. The erection of the statues of military men in London, says Spurgeon, reveals 'the trickery of an ignorant age, the gewgaws of a people that loved bloodshed despite their profession of religion'. He looks forward to the day when Nelson will be pulled down from his column and replaced by a statue of George Whitefield, and the iron and brass of every statue standing in the city will be sold 'and the price thereof cast at the apostles' feet, that they may make distribution as every man hath need'.

Scottish paintings

But to return to Edinburgh. Our search for distinctive features of Scottish culture might, naturally enough, take us inside the National Gallery where, among some wonderful Scottish paintings, we find J.H. Lorimer's work 'Ordination of Elders'. This picture, which captures the moment at which local worthies are inducted into office by the minister of the kirk, offers a further indicator of the significance of Protestant Christianity in Scotland; more specifically, it points to the influence of Presbyterianism and Calvinism and again reminds us of the role of the Bible in this culture. John Philip's painting 'Presbyterian Catechising' carries the same message.

Similar pictures can be found in galleries across Scotland. In the Dundee City Museum there is a delightful canvas by R. McGregor bearing the title 'The Story of the Flood', illustrating the way in which the formal teaching of the church was backed up by an informal instruction at the level of the home. The same museum contains exhibits illustrating the life and work of another Scottish evangelical missionary whose remarkable work in West Africa is celebrated in a stained glass window—the redoubtable Mary Slessor.

The Aberdeen Art Gallery displays a huge canvas by Sir Edwin Landseer which suggests why the story of the flood might have a special resonance in the Highlands. This large canvas shows the pain and dislocation suffered by poor families during a devastating flood in the Highlands. Although it has no particular religious significance, it does introduce us to another very powerful set of images often used to delineate Scottish culture: the land of mountain and flood, of tartan, kilts and heather. Incidentally, there is a connection between this painting and the honouring of British war heroes in London so deplored by Spurgeon: Landseer was the artist responsible for the huge lions which guard the foot of Nelson's column in Trafalgar Square.

Composers

Let us make one more stop in our Edinburgh quest for an understanding of Scottish culture. We turn out of Princes Street and walk up to the Usher Hall. It is perfectly possible that the evening concert there commences with an overture by Hamish MacCunn entitled, 'Land of the Mountain and Flood'. This brilliant music was written by a young man only eighteen years of age and gave expression to the composer's sense of pride in Scotland. In fact the second half of the nineteenth century witnessed a great surge of distinctively Scottish music: Alexander Mackenzie's 'Scottish Rhapsody', John Blackwood McEwen's 'Solway Symphony', the patriotic symphonic poems of William Wallace, and the 'Celtic' and 'Hebridean' Symphonies of Granville

Bantock. In all these works (which are only now beginning to be appreciated after years of neglect) there is an evocation of the glories of rural Scotland. There is also, especially in Bantock, a typically romantic desire to recover ancient pre-Christian traditions, to return to what is believed to be the 'Gaelic vision'. One of Bantock's works is called the 'Pagan Symphony'.

Geographic identity
Having concluded this brief survey of public art in Edinburgh we are in a position to identify two of the strands which contribute to the making of Scottish cultural identity. In the first place, the question 'What is Scotland?' can be answered geograpically. It is a territory, a place which can be identified on the map of the British Isles, and an area whose beauty has been depicted in literature, music, photography and, not least, by the tourist industry. The sense of belonging to a particular place is an important dimension in the creation of cultural identity; it has nurtured and sustained Scottish national pride while also significantly shaping perceptions of Scotland in the wider world.

However, we need to be aware of the possibility that the presentation of Scotland as 'land of mountain and flood' can involve a selective approach to historical realities. The comment of John Prebble on the emptiness of the Highlands is unforgettable: 'In all of Britain only among [the Scottish hills] can one find real solitude and if their history is known there is no satisfaction to be got from the experience.' He goes on to say that 'while the rest of Scotland was permitting the expulsion of its Highland people it was also forming that romantic attachment to kilt and tartan that scarcely compensates for the disappearance of a race to whom such things were once commonplace reality' (Prebble:1969,8). These moving words suggest that there is substance in the warning expressed by Neal Ascherson: 'We talk easily about the forging of a nation, but forgery has played a real part in the foundation and revival of many nations.' [1]

2. Calvinism and the Reformation

The second influence on Scottish culture which is evident from a casual walk down Princes Street relates to the religious tradition stemming from the Reformation. Symbolic reminders of the importance of the Calvinist vision of a godly commonwealth in which the whole life of the nation was to be permeated by biblical values are to be found throughout Scotland.

William Storrar observes that the original motto of the city of Glasgow—'Let Glasgow Flourish By The Preaching of the Word of God and the Praising of His Name' – reflects Knox's vision of national reformation and encapsulates the unique Scottish religiouscultural ethos. The Edinburgh statues of Chalmers and Guthrie are important reminders of a time when evangelical Calvinism had a profound impact on the culture, while the public recognition of missionaries like Livingstone and Mary Slessor bears witness to the fact that Scotland provided a base from which a world-transformative Christianity spread around the globe.

Chalmers and Guthrie

I want to dwell briefly on the significance of the ministries of Chalmers and Guthrie. I suggest that these men are important in relation to our subject precisely because their work was done during the floodtide of early modernisation, when the forces unleashed by the Enlightenment and the industrial revolution challenged both the validity and the viability of the social vision of the Scottish Reformation.

Chalmers moved from rural Fife to a city experiencing the kind of explosive growth in population which is today reported in the burgeoning urban centres of Africa, South America, and Asia. By the middle of the nineteenth century the population of Glasgow had increased twelvefold since 1775; it was almost to treble again by 1911. Guthrie arrived in Edinburgh from Tayside and discovered a situation which, according to an observer, left every visitor with two impressions: 'a sense of [Edinburgh's] extraordinary beauty and a horror of its unspeakable filth'.

Here are the ambiguities of modernisation: increasing wealth side by side with grinding poverty, the transformation of the material conditions for human existence, accompanied by the fragmentation of society and the erosion of human dignity and worth. What lessons can we learn from Chalmers and Guthrie as they wrestled with such issues at a time of massive cultural change in Scotland?

Both men were of course oustandingly gifted preachers. Some years back I chanced upon two volumes of Chalmers' Lectures on the Epistle to the Romans in a second-hand bookshop and was astonished to discover the freshness and originality of his exposition across a gap of well over a century. Reading sermons like these, one realizes why thoughtful people wrestling with new challenges to faith in an era of rapid and profoundly disturbing intellectual and social change found Chalmers' sermons so helpful. His preaching was magnetic among the urban middle classes. His constant and passionate insistence that the possession of wealth brought huge responsibilities 'was an inspiration to generations of soulsearching men to give generously of their money and time'.[2]

Guthrie was scarcely less able as a preacher. His powers of oratory were legendary and could stir deep emotions. On one occasion he described a disaster at sea in such vivid terms that a sailor in the congregation leapt up and removed his coat, ready to plunge in to save the drowning.

Political conservatism

However, there were significant differences between these men when it came to cultural analysis and the application of the Gospel to socioeconomic problems. Chalmers' political conservatism is well known. He absolved what he called 'the wealthier orders of society' from all responsibility for the degradation of the urban poor and defended the social *status quo* on the grounds that, 'The structure of human society admits of no other arrangement.'

Speaking to working-class parishioners in Glasgow, Chalmers lavished praise on a social order in which the monarchy was 'borne up by a splendid aristocracy, and a gradation of ranks shelving downwards toward the basement of society'.[3] He was equally uncritical in his advocacy of laissez-faire economics, committing himself to the extraordinary claim that selfishness 'is the grand principle on which the brotherhood of the human race is made to hang together'.[4]   Statements like these led to Chalmers gaining the doubtful distinction of being (as far as I can discover) the only Scottish evangelical singled out for attack in the writings of Karl Marx.[5]

New thoughts and fresh solutions

Dr Guthrie's approach is very different. His remarkable book *The City – Its Sins and Its Sorrows* reveals a deeply compassionate man who is able to think new thoughts and seek fresh solutions. Guthrie's analysis of the social injustices which threatened the cohesion and stability of Scotland is both lucid and passionate. Using modern terminology one could argue that Guthrie recognises both the structural dimensions of evil, and that he writes with a 'bias toward the poor'. He argues, for example, that the destitute classes of Glasgow and Edinburgh are doubly deprived of justice for, on the one hand, they live in conditions of such squalor that they are driven to seek food by any means possible, while on the other hand, respectable society exacts retribution from them for crimes which are traceable to its own heartlessness and indifference: 'we first condemn them to crime, and then condemn them to punishment. And where is the justice of that?'[6]   Guthrie asks equally searching questions concerning economics: he attacks 'a system of trade which offers up our children in sacrifice to the Moloch of money and builds fortunes in many instances on the ruins of public morality and domestic happiness'.

The contrasting responses of these two great preachers to the problems resulting from the impact of modernisation suggests that evangelical religion can take very different forms. It can buttress the status quo, offering a religious justification for things as they are, and so become an ideology. Or it can function as a counter-culture, exposing injustice and offering a radically different vision of human society from the perspective of the Gospel. As Scottish Christians face the challenges of bearing witness to Christ in a situation of renewed cultural flux brought about by the collapse of modernity, it is well to recall the contrasting aspects of their tradition, symbolized by the two Edinburgh statues.

II. The 20th Century

I want now to return to the present and consider the forces shaping
Scottish culture today. Dr Guthrie died in 1873 at a time when
traditional Christianity seemed under increasing threat. In an age
of widespread religious doubt Scotland produced some notable
apologists, not least James Denney and James Orr. However, in
the twentieth century it was the Enlightenment tradition that came
under increasing threat as the benefits of a scientific worldview
came to be questioned and the grand promise of universal
happiness proved a mirage.

The term 'postmodern' is a recent invention, but it now seems
obvious that the credibility of the culture of modernity has been
eroded over a long period of time. Anyone who doubts this should
read Eric Hobsbawm's history of the twentieth century, *Age of
Extremes*. This important book is prefaced with a series of
quotations in which well-known people assess the twentieth
century. The late Isaiah Berlin comments, 'I remember it only as
the most terrible century in Western history.' William Golding
suggests it has been 'the most violent century in human history',
while Yehudi Menuhin observes that the twentieth century 'raised
the greatest hopes ever conceived by humanity, and destroyed all
illusions and ideals'.[7]

The ambiguities and tensions of modernity, already evident in
the nineteenth century, have become more and more obvious and
painful. Modern man can walk on the moon and explore the depths
of the cosmos, but he seems powerless to prevent the evils of
genocide in Bosnia or Rwanda, or of infanticide in Liverpool,
Dunblane or Belgium. To be modern, writes Marshall Berman, is
'to experience personal and social life as a maelstrom, to find
one's world and oneself in perpetual disintegration and renewal,
trouble and anguish, ambiguity and contradiction: to be part of a
universe in which all that is solid melts into air'.[8] If at the end of
the nineteenth century there were growing numbers of people who
found it difficult to believe in God, the problem now has become
how to continue to believe in man.

Modern cultural symbols

How has this general cultural crisis in the Western world affected Scotland? We should perhaps remember here that Glasgow's motto, so characteristic of the Reformed vision of a godly society, was truncated to become a materialist slogan—'Let Glasgow Flourish'. So far as Edinburgh is concerned, the really powerful cultural symbols are now located on the opposite side of Princes Street to Dr Guthrie's statue. In a recent survey of 7000 people in six countries, 88 percent identified the corporate symbol of the McDonald's hamburger chain while only 54 percent could explain the significance of the Christian cross. No contemporary cultural analysis can ignore the forces of global capitalism, symbolised by the illuminated shopfronts of Marks and Spencer, Disney, Virgin Records and McDonalds, which increasingly shape Scottish culture, as they do cultures around the world.

Clearly then, an understanding of Scottish culture informed solely by the romantic perception of the Highlands or by the religious traditions of the past is bound to be partial, if not fundamentally misleading. This is an important point for Christians outside Scotland, since one can still find people who express the belief that 'real' religion is to be found at the Celtic 'peripheries' of the British Isles. Believers struggling with the consequences of the erosion of a living and public faith at the metropolitan centre may seek solace in a romantic notion that pure traditions of Reformed Christianity, or revivalism, or even Celtic holism, remain intact and unsullied by modernity in the Highlands. But to depict modern Scotland as the 'Land of Reformers and Covenanters' is to construct a romantic myth no less misleading than certain versions of the 'Land of mountain and flood' story. To illustrate this I want to take brief notice of some examples of modern Scottish art, music and literature.

Art

Let us consider two pictures which hang in the Museum of Modern Art in Edinburgh. Ken Currie's 'Glasgow Triptych: Template of the Future' depicts, according to the artist, the decline of the radical socialist tradition which has been a significant force in modern Scotland. Currie's painting shows an old man slumped in a

Glasgow bar, drowning his sorrows in the realization that genuine social transformation will not come about through radical political action. At the centre of the picture a young boy plays with a model of a black aircraft, an ominous symbol of the violence of mechanized warfare soon to engulf and divide Europe.

The second painting is Peter Howson's 'Just Another Bloody Saturday', which deals with a rather different form of substitute religion which has had considerable salience in Scotland: professional football. Commenting on the rise of football clubs in nineteenth century Scotland, T.C. Smout observes that the game seemed to arouse exactly the heart-warming zeal and total devotion which ministers of the gospel 'had tried so hard, so painfully and so totally unsuccessfully to arouse for God'.9 Howson's canvas though, with its disturbing portrayal of a baying crowd, depicts terrible anger rather than zeal; whatever enjoyment there may be in this Saturday afternoon escape from everyday reality, it seems as empty and insubstantial as the artificial light streaming from floodlight pylons which are the only sources of illumination in the picture.

Music
So far as the contemporary music scene is concerned, Scotland has produced a number of thoughtful rock bands whose lyrics express the same erosion of hope and the sense of human lostness so movingly depicted on the canvasses in the Museum of Modern Art. In so far as such groups express convictions that are widespread among the present generation, they challenge the romantic myths concerning Scottish culture to which reference has been made earlier. Take the song 'Nothing Ever Happens' from the group Del Amitri:

Post office clerks put up signs saying position closed
And secretaries turn off typewriters and put on their coats

Janitors padlock the gates
For security guards to patrol,
And bachelors phone up their friends for a drink
While the married ones turn on a chat show

And they'll all be lonely tonight and lonely tomorrow
Gentleman time please, you know we can't serve anymore
Now the traffic lights turn to stop, when there's nothing to go
And by five o'clock everything's dead
And every third car is a cab,
And ignorant people sleep in their beds
Like the doped white mice in a college lab

Nothing ever happens, nothing happens at all,
The needle returns to the start of the song
And we all sing along like before

And we'll all be lonely tonight and lonely tomorrow
Bill hoardings advertise products that nobody needs
While angry from Manchester writes to complain about
All the repeats on TV
And computer terminals report some gains
On the value of copper and tin
While American businessmen snap up Van Goghs
For the price of a hospital wing

Nothing ever happens, nothing happens at all
The needle returns to the start of the song
And we all sing along like before
Nothing ever happens, nothing happens at all
They'll burn down the synagogue at six o' clock
And we'll all go along like before

And we'll all be lonely tonight and lonely tomorrow

A sense of the emptiness of human life in a culture in which
God is no longer known is yet more evident in the lyrics of a
group bearing the name The Lost Soul Band:

D'you think God has changed with the times?
Does he understand restless feelings?
Does he understand mine?
Does he know half the world doesn't pray anymore?
Does he know half the people don't quite know what to say anymore?

Literature

It is beyond the scope of this paper to provide a detailed survey of Scottish literature but many recent works of fiction bear testimony to the tragedy of life in the godless wastelands of our times. In a fascinating article on contemporary Scottish literature Beth Dickson has examined a series of modern novels, comparing them with classical works like Scott's *Old Mortality* and James Hogg's *Justified Sinner*. Commenting on James Kelman's *The Bus Conductor Hines* she notes, 'The only remnants of Christianity in the world he describes are a few of the names of God repeatedly taken in vain.' After discussing the work of Kelman, Alasdair Gray, and William McIlvanney, she concludes, 'A working knowledge of Christianity has disappeared.'[10]

On my last visit to Waterstones in Princes Street I purchased a book with the title *Life After God*. This is not Scottish fiction (the author is a Canadian), but it records with almost brutal honesty the sheer boredom of postmodern life. On the penultimate page Douglas Coupland makes this remarkable confession:

> Now – here is my secret: I tell it to you with an openness of heart that I doubt I shall ever achieve again, so I pray that you are in a quiet room as you hear these words. My secret is that I need God – that I am sick and can no longer make it alone. I need God to help me give, because I no longer seem capable of giving; to help me be kind, as I no longer seem capable of kindness; to help me love, as I seem beyond being able to love.[11]

What are the implications of this brief survey of contemporary culture for the mission of the church in Scotland today? I would like to identify three issues, framed in the form of questions, that seem unavoidable in regard to mission in Scotland's changing society.

III. Three Questions

What is the future of the pulpit?

First, what is the future of the pulpit in Scotland given the fact that in the wider culture communication increasingly takes place by means of visual symbols? As the Edinburgh statues have shown, the preaching of the Word of God has been absolutely central within the Scottish religious tradition since the Reformation. The Dictionary of Scottish Church History and Theology contains long articles on 'Preachers' and 'Preaching', detailing the amazing consistency and richness of this tradition.

I hope I do not exaggerate when I say that at times within the Reformed tradition the sermon became almost synonymous with the act of worship itself. Thus, the gathering of the congregation for worship was known as 'the time of the sermon', or 'the time of prayers and preaching'. A tradition in which the preached Word is so central faces some difficult questions today: can traditional preaching survive in an era of multi-channel TV, the global spread of new information technologies, and a shift in education from texts to images, from books to screens?

Warnings

Before attempting to answer that question we may note that the problems of preaching in the context of modernity have long been noted. In 1946 a prisoner of war returning home commented on attending church that it seemed as though a glass cover had been placed over the pulpit. 'This smothers all sound. Around the pulpit our contemporaries are standing. They too talk, and they call. But on the inside this is not understood. The glass cover smothers all sound. Thus we still see each other talk, but we don't understand each other anymore.'

The great German preacher Helmut Thielicke wrote at length on the post-war crisis facing the Reformation tradition of preaching. Ministers invariably seemed to perform their public ministry 'almost to the exclusion of any public notice whatsoever'. There was, he said, a 'tremendous contradiction' between the conviction that they are called to proclaim a message that would revolutionise life and, on the other hand, the 'utter immovability of the deeply rutted tracks in which they must move'.12 Thielicke lamented the chasm that existed between the pulpit and the everyday world of those who still chose to sit beneath it. Sermons so often betrayed the fact that ministerial life seemed to isolate preachers within an archaic culture shaped by Christendom, leaving congregations unable to make any connection between what was heard from the puplit and the struggles, dilemmas and questions arising from daily life in a secular culture.

Thielicke's warnings suggest that if we wish to answer my question concerning the future of preaching by a ringing affirmation of its non-negotiability as the means of Christian communication, we will still need to look seriously at the style and content of the sermon. However sound the exegesis of Scripture may be, unless there is dynamic, living contact between the message of the Bible and the world in which men, women and young people actually live and work, then Thielicke's prediction of the death of preaching will be fulfilled.

The electronic superhighway

However, I do not think this response goes far enough. Not for a moment do I wish to deny the place of powerful preaching in the purposes of God; I believe gifted expositors who possess a deep understanding of contemporary realities may still break into modern culture with a message of hope, reconciliation and freedom. At the same time, we dare not ignore the shifts that have taken place in this culture as the result of the massive technological changes in recent times.

Many analysts believe that we are living through a cultural transformation at least as significant as that which occurred with the invention of the printing press in the sixteenth century. That invention facilitated a transition from oral and visual forms of communication to a culture shaped by printed texts. Luther seized the opportunities created by this new technology to such an extent that it is impossible to think of the spread of the Reformation apart from Gutenberg's printing press.

My question is simple: why should the church at the close of the twentieth century not employ the new technologies now shaping our culture for the sake of the kingdom of God? Why should the electronic superhighway not become a 'way of the Lord'? It is simply impossible to reply that the Bible sanctions nothing but preaching as the means of Christian communication.

The Bible does nothing of the sort; it is far from being limited in this way to a single channel of communication. From Genesis to Revelation we find an infinitely rich variety of communication, including story, dream, proverb, vision, as well as sermon. It is a biblical text that affirms 'Ears that hear and eyes that see – the Lord has made them both' (Prov. 20:12). In an era when, whether we like it or not, our childrens' lives are being shaped by visual imagery through TV, film and video, Scottish Christians cannot afford to ignore the implications of this proverb.

The future of the church in Scotland?
My second question is this: what is the future of the church in Scotland, given that the culture is now religiously plural? As we have seen, for many people in modern Scotland, notwithstanding the spiritual glories of the Reformation and the revivals in the past, even the memory of God has now faded. The vacuum left by the decline of institutional Christianity is filled by a bewildering variety of beliefs, whether these are secular substitutes for religion, or various non-Christian faiths. I have met policemen in Aberdeen who swear by the I Ching, and had long discussions on a train out of Edinburgh with a teacher who described his personal spiritual quests at Findhorn.

In this changed cultural context, the ideology of Christendom, the belief that in some sense Scotland remains a Christian nation, actually forms a barrier to the fulfillment of the church's missionary calling. The 'glass cover' described earlier has become a distorting mirror, blinding believers to the realities of a deeply secular and pluralist society, while presenting unbelievers with an image of Christianity that is a travesty of the revolutionary community described in the pages of the New Testament. Kierkegaard was surely correct when he said that Christendom removed the offence, the paradox, from the Gospel and so transformed Christianity into something entirely different from what it is in the book of the Acts of the Apostles.

A defunct ideology

Is it not obvious that the longer Christians cling to the fiction of Christendom and allow their approach to witness and evangelism to be shaped by this defunct ideology, the greater the danger that the Christian faith will die away in large parts of Scotland. This point has been made very clearly by William Storrar in his groundbreaking book, *Scottish Identity: A Christian Vision.* He calls the Church of Scotland to abandon its pretensions to be the national church in order to become a confessing, witnessing community. The absence of missionary assumptions in the Reformed view of the church has led to a deep crisis for the Kirk because it has 'hung on to a view of its identity which looks increasingly shipwrecked in the secular tides of the late twentieth century'.

There must be a fundamental shift from being the Church of Scotland to becoming the church for Scotland. The Kirk must 're-think its Christian identity as the community of those who confess Jesus as Lord, with a distinctive life from the rest of the secular community and yet with an overriding sense of responsibility for that nation in mission, social criticism and service'.[13]

Renewal and liberation

This prophetic call to mission has a resonance far beyond the Church of Scotland. Other denominational traditions, including those which have formally dissented from the established Church, have been influenced by the Christendom model in all kinds of ways. For example, the appeals made in evangelistic services among the Baptists or the Plymouth Brethren invariably assume a knowledge of God and an underlying familiarity with the Gospel story, which suggests that the so-called 'free' churches are as distant from social reality as the Church of Scotland. The urgent need therefore is for the whole people of God in Scotland to be renewed in unity, truth and love, to shake off the chains which still bind them to an outmoded and unbiblical conception of the church, and be liberated to engage in authentic, costly service in mission in the context of Scotland's changing culture.

Pseudo-religious nationalism

In relation to Christian witness in modern Scotland, it is impossible to avoid some comment on the constitutional issue. I speak here with considerable caution and reserve but some observations from an Englishman living two miles south of the border may be helpful. Actually, living beside the border between two nations is an interesting experience. I have often recalled the profound observation of the Russian poet, Yevtushenko: 'I suppose that in the beginning men defined borders and then borders began to define men.' It is a comment that warns us of the great danger of a nationalism that becomes idolatrous.

Given the condition of Scottish culture as we have described it, there is a very real possibility that people lacking a transcendent reference point for their lives make the love of nation a new locus of the sacred. Christians on both sides of the border need to he very alert to the dangers of a pseudo-religious nationalism which makes demands that no disciple of Christ can possibly concede.

At the same time, it is surely legitimate for men to 'define borders'. That is to say, socio-political structures are not absolutes; they belong within the sphere of human culture and are open to discussion, critical analysis and change. In a shifting historical and cultural context, rigid political structures may suppress entirely legitimate human aspirations and, at worst become oppressive. I fear that the social conservatism of Thomas Chalmers and William Wilberforce at a critical juncture in British social history may have actually accelerated the process by which our culture became secularised.

It matters a great deal where Christians come down in the argument, when, at crucial points in history, there are opportunities to enact social change which could lead to a more just ordering of society. This being so, it is imperative that Scottish Christians contribute to the current debate concerning Scottish identity. Indeed, I hope that such discussions north of the border may stimulate a long overdue engagement in serious theological reflection in the south on what it means to be English.

The nature of mission today?
My third and final question is this: what is the nature of mission
in a culture that is both postmodern and post-Christian?

A recent conference raised the question 'Death or Glory?' in
relation to the church's mission in modern Scotland. I suggest
this is actually a false choice since 'glory' is not really an option
for believers on this side of heaven. Of course there are 'glimpses
of glory' and the lives of Christians should reflect the glory
revealed in Christ, the suffering servant of God. But throughout
the long era of Christendom 'glory' has been a problem; a church
identified with power and privilege has too often subverted the
Gospel and abandoned the call to mission. Mission in a culture
pervaded by nihilistic hopelessness and by increasing levels of
violence requires a humble and penitent church prepared to face
rejection and suffering. Even as this paper was being written the
murder of Christopher Gray outside his parish church in Liverpool
vividly illustrated the point. In a moving tribute entitled 'Sense of
Mission', Adrian Hastings quoted an essay published by this young
pastor just before he was killed: ministers, he said, need to 'be
like Christ in the faithful service of their flocks; even to the point
of sacrificing their own lives'.[14]

Authentic ministry
Unless Christian witness is to be confined to the relative security
of comfortable suburbs, we will need a generation of men and
women who hear the call of Christ to authentic apostolic ministry
involving costly service and real personal risk. If this call to mission
is refused, if we remain in captivity to a culture wedded to the
worship of mammon, continuing to delude ourselves and others
that this culture is in some sense 'Christian', then the church in
Scotland really will face death. Christianity may survive as a
privatized religion providing a warm glow to a minority who opt
for it, but as a living, world-transformative faith it will have become
extinguished. The light will have gone out.

In this scenario serious social criticism may be left to Muslims,
who often perceive all too clearly the entanglement of Christianity
with Western materialism and find it impossible to take our

God-talk seriously. Sociologists like Steve Bruce have suggested that we are already well down the path that leads to the death of socially significant religion; they argue that all the evidence shows that whatever value evangelical conversion may have in the lives of individuals, its cultural significance is increasingly marginalized.

Death or Glory? While the crisis facing Christianity in the West in general, and in Scotland in particular is desperately real, it also presents us with a unique opportunity, a *kairos*. At this critical point we may return to first principles, recovering the Gospel and learning afresh what it means to be the disciples of Christ in a hostile environment. But the opportunites may not last long and the issues which require to be faced if we are to rise to challenge of mission in Scotland's changing culture need to be placed at the top of our agendas.

Bibliography

I would like to acknowledge the help received in writing this paper from Professors Steve Bruce and Donald Meek of the University of Aberdeen. Professor Bruce offered me some helpful observations at an early stage and generously provided me with some of his own materials on the subject of religion in modern Scotland. My friend Donald Meek read the final draft of the paper at a late stage and offered helpful and encouraging comments. Responsibility for what is written here remains, of course, entirely my own.

Neil Ascherson, 'The Religion of Nationalism' *The Observer, 4.12.88*.

David Bebbington, 'Scottish Cultural Influences on Evangelicalism', *Scottish Bulletin of Evangelical Theology* (Spring 1996,14/1),p.23-36.

Marshall Berman, *All That Is Solid Melts Into Air: The Experience of Modernity* (London, Verso, 1982).

Steve Bruce, *No Pope of Rome: Militant Protestantism in Modern Scotland* (Edinburgh, Mainstream Publishing, 1985).

Steve Bruce, 'A Failure of the Imagination: Ethnicity and Nationalism in Modern Scotland', *Scotia*, XVII, 1993, p.1-16.

Nigel M. de S. Cameron (ed), *Dictionary of Scottish Church History and Theology* (Edinburgh, T & T Clark, 1993).

Thomas Chalmers,*The Application of Christianity to the Commercial and Ordinary Affairs of Life* (Glasgow, Chalmers & Collins, 1820).

John Coleman & Milo Tomka (eds),*Religion and Nationalism* (London, SCM Press, 1995).

Beth Dickson, 'The Gospel and Scottish Fiction',*Scottish Bulletin of Evangelical Theology* (Spring 1996, 14/1), p.51-64.

Jacques Ellul, *The Subversion of Christianity* (Grand Rapids, Eerdmans, 1986).

Thomas Guthrie,*The City—its Sins and Its Sorrows* (Edinburgh, Adam and Charles Black, 1857).

Adrian Hastings, 'Sense of Mission'*The Guardian*, 15 August 1996 p.13.

Eric Hobsbawm, *Age of Extremes* (Abacus, London, 1995).

J. C. Hoekendijk,*The Church Inside Out* (London,SCM Press, 1964).

J. D. Mackie, *A History of the Scottish Reformation* (Edinburgh, Church of Scotland, 1960).

N. Masterman (ed), *Chalmers on Charity* (London, Constable, 1900).

David McCrone,*Understanding Scotland: The Sociology of a Stateless Nation* (London,Routledge, 1992).

Donald Meek, 'Saints and Scarecrows: The Churches and Gaelic Culture in the Highlands Since 1560',*Scottish Bulletin of Evangelical Theology* (Spring 1996, 14/1) p.322.

John Prebble, *The Highland Clearances* (Harmondsworth, Penguin, 1969).

T. C.Smout, *A Century of the Scottish People: 1830-1950* (London, Fontana Press, 1987).

William Storrar, *Scottish Identity: A Christian Vision* (Edinburgh, The Handsel Press, 1990).

Helmut Thielicke, *The Trouble With The Church: A Call for Revival* (London, Hodder,1965).

Gene E. Veith, *Guide To Contemporary Culture* (Leicester, Crossway Books, 1994)

Graham Walker & Tom Gallagher (eds), *Sermons and Battle Hymns: Protestant Popular Culture in Modern Scotland* (Edinburgh, University Press, 1990).

Antonie Wessels, *Europe: Was It Ever Really Christian?* (London, SCM Press, 1994).

Antonie Wessels,*Secularised Europe: Who Will Carry Off Its Soul?* (Geneva, WCC Publications, 1996).

Notes

1. N. Ascherson, 'The Religion of Nationalism', *The Observer*, 4 December 1988.

2. T. C. Smout, *A Century of the Scottish People: 1830-1950* (Fontana Press, London, 1987), p. 186.

3. N. Masterman (ed), *Chalmers on Charity* (Constable, London, 1900), pp.167-95.

4. Thomas Chalmers, *The Application of Christianity to the Commercial and Ordinary Affairs of Life* (Chalmers & Collins, Glasgow, 1820), p. 76.

5. [But see the references in chapter 2 to Chalmers' practical measures to combat poverty – Editor]

6. Thomas Guthrie, *The City – Its Sins and Its Sorrows* (Adam and Charles Black, Edinburgh, 1857), p.80.

7. Eric Hobsbawm, *Age of Extremes* (Abacus, London,1995), pp.1-2.

8. Marshall Berman, *All That Is Solid Melts Into Air: The Experience of Modernity* (Verso, London, 1982), p.345.

9. T. C. Smout, op. cit. p.202.

10. Beth Dickson, 'The Gospel and Scottish Fiction', *Scottish Bulletin of Evangelical Theology* (Spring 1996,14/1), pp.62-3.

11. Douglas Coupland, *Life After God* (Touchsone Books, London,1994), p.359.

12. Helmut Thielicke, *The Trouble With The Church: A Call For Revival* (Hodder, London,1965) p. 1-2.

13. William Storrar, *Scottish Identity: A Christian Vision* (Handsel Press, Edinburgh,1990), pp.134 & 223.

14. Adrian Hastings, 'Sense of Mission', *The Guardian,* 15 August 1996.

Chapter 2

Mission in Scotland, 1846-1946

D. W. Bebbington

The Victorian Period

'It is highly gratifying to contemplate the recent indications we have of the ascendancy of religious feeling and Christian philanthropic enterprise in our land, in such as, the institution of the Evangelical Alliance...'[1]

These are not the words of a florid commentator on events of the 1990s, but those of Thomas Rosie, secretary of the undenominational East Coast Mission, written in 1858 about recent developments. He gave pride of place to the formation of the Evangelical Alliance in 1846. That was by no means the only major ecclesiastical happening in Scotland during the 1840s. In 1843 there had taken place the Disruption, when the Free Church under Thomas Chalmers broke away from the Church of Scotland, perhaps the most important event in nineteenth-century Scottish history. On the same day in 1843 James Morison led in the creation of the Evangelical Union, so separating from the United Secession Church. And in the same year three evangelical congregations, the one in Edinburgh having David Drummond as its minister, left the Scottish Episcopal Church. Evangelical stirrings were undermining existing structures: new wine was breaking old bottles. Conversely in 1847, the United Secession Church and the Relief Church combined as the United Presbyterian Church on the ground of their common Evangelicalism. As the Evangelical Alliance itself also showed, evangelical religion was clearly a bond as well as a separator.

In 1851, five years after the foundation of the Evangelical

Alliance, there took place the only government census of religion ever conducted in Britain. Attendances in Scotland as a proportion of the total population were roughly 26% at morning worship, 17% in the afternoon and 5% in the evening.[2] If allowance is made for those who attended twice or even three times, something like 35% of the Scottish people were in church on census Sunday. That figure compares very favourably with the proportion of the adult Scottish population at worship in 1994, which was 14%.[3] The denominational distribution is instructive. The Church of Scotland retained only 32% of worshippers in the wake of the Disruption, while as high a proportion as 59% attended other Presbyterian churches and 9% belonged to non-Presbyterian denominations.[4] Whereas in the early eighteenth century the Church of Scotland, the national church, had enjoyed the support of the vast majority of the population, by the mid-nineteenth century it was in a minority. The census revealed a pattern of religious fragmentation. It explains a great deal of why church leaders felt the need of an Evangelical Alliance, a body designed to draw together those in different denominations but like-minded on the subject of the gospel.

Church growth

What was the pattern of church growth from the 1840s onwards? All evangelical denominations, without exception, increased their numbers over the remaining years of the century, as, of course, did the Roman Catholic Church, whose ranks were swelled by throngs of Irish immigrants from the 1840s. Church adherence overall, based on membership or active involvement together with Sunday school enrolment, all relative to population, has been calculated to have reached its peak in around 1905.[5] At that point over half the Scottish people belonged to some Christian body. Thereafter the proportion began to fall, though at first very slowly. Consequently the Victorian period has to be seen as a success story for the Scottish churches, overwhelmingly evangelical in this era. What explains their degree of success in mission? It was not that there were no obstacles; rather it was because their energy triumphed over the problems that confronted them. It will be useful to consider the obstacles before moving on to the reasons for growth among Victorian evangelicals.

Obstacles to mission

First among the difficulties was *the problem of poverty*. There were many reports of slum-dwellers saying they could not go to church because they could not afford Sunday clothes. It was a period when the standard of living for the agricultural worker was often barely an improvement on pre-industrial times. Industrial workers themselves commonly suffered from bouts of unemployment in periods of recession. Yet the normal system of raising church finance was by pew rents. Seats would be let by the quarter and paid for in advance. Although some prices were low, even they could not be afforded by many, especially those uncertain of a regular income. There were normally seats reserved for the poor, but they were located in unattractive spots such as draughty corners and, like the Poor Law, carried an enormous burden of social stigma.[6] Some congregations turned instead to other methods of fund-raising, but the process was slow and damage was done to the appeal of the churches.

A second obstacle was *the public house*. Alcohol consumption was high and rising until the 1870s. There were numerous drink outlets: in 1851 there was one for every 164 inhabitants in Edinburgh, and one for every 163 in Glasgow. There had been more drink licensees in Glasgow in 1830 than all other food sellers altogether. From the 1828 Licensing Act the sale of alcohol was prohibited during the hours of worship, but licensed premises were open immediately afterwards and had been open the night before.[7] Many people were as unfit to attend the morning service as the afternoon service. It was not just that public houses competed with the churches for the time of their patrons. The bar was an alternative focus of sociability to the church, the centre of a different, rough culture. Bar and church were self-conscious rivals. Thus at Portknockie, Banff, during the revival of 1859-60 two publicans removed their signboards, a gesture expressing the victory of the gospel over strong drink.[8] The public house represented a standing challenge to the churches for the loyalty of the people.

Popular culture, thirdly, was an obstacle to the progress of the gospel. Evangelists threatened traditional ways with their denunciation of occasions of sin such as town fairs. Resistance sprang up in defence of the folk ways of the community. Thus at Inverurie in 1871, a campaign by the Northern Evangelistic Society was interrupted on the second evening by thirty locals who shouted continuously and at the end tried to assault the preachers.[9] Popular culture was made the more resistant to the gospel by its interweaving with residual pagan superstition. Preachers in the Highlands found the people attached to customs such as leaving gifts at springs, a relic of devotion to water spirits. Nor did this alternative species of religiosity disappear in urban areas. Addiction to lucky charms persisted in the largest British cities throughout the nineteenth century and beyond.[10] It was hard to draw folk away from the web of traditional customs that bound them.

It is sometimes suggested that a fourth factor, *secularism,* was responsible for undermining faith during the nineteenth century. In Prussia, for instance, there were militant atheists who fostered popular anticlericalism on a large scale. The equivalent phenomenon was remarkably weak in Britain. The National Secular Society covering the whole of the United Kingdom possessed in 1880 near its peak no more than 6,000 members.[11] There were occasional, if spectacular, local debates organised by visiting secularist speakers, but little popular disbelief of a militant kind. Atheism could not rank alongside poverty, public houses and popular culture as a reason for avoiding Christian influence.

Evangelism in rural areas

The explanations of missionary achievement may begin with the impact of the churches on the countryside. Especially in tight-knit lowland parishes, traditional churchgoing was encouraged by many lairds and heritors as a matter of deference. Such social pressure from above would normally benefit the established church, though there were numerous Episcopal and Catholic instances as well, but social pressure from one's peers to attend church, another potent force in the countryside, might also be exerted in favour of the

Free Church once it had established its credentials to be a part of community life. Rural churchgoing undoubtedly grew in the Victorian era. There had been a notable lack of places of worship, especially in the vast parishes of the Highlands where the single church might be inaccessible to a majority of the inhabitants. Although the undivided Church of Scotland had taken up the problem in the 1820s, the Disruption produced the greatest remedy by creating a desire in the Free Church, as a shadow establishment, to erect a place of worship in every parish. There was therefore much church building in the Highlands in the 1840s. Between 1841 and 1851 the number of church sittings there and in the Hebrides went up from 240 per 1000 inhabitants to 474 per 1000, a virtual doubling of the provision.[12] These institutional efforts were supplemented by the work of itinerant preachers, most of them Independent or Baptist, who travelled huge distances to proclaim the gospel.[13] But it was the Free Church that won the hearts of the people. By the 1880s it possessed the allegiance of an absolute majority of the inhabitants of the bulk of the Highlands.[14] Mission proved effective in the countryside.

Towns and cities

The same is true in the towns and cities. T. C. Smout's rightly influential digest, *A Century of the Scottish People, 1830-1950*, contrasts the godly countryside with the large towns where religion was decaying.[15] It reflects a body of historical literature published between the 1950s and 1970s that emphasised the failure of the churches in the nineteenth-century era of urbanisation. The authors tended to take the laments of ministers about absences from worship at face value, forgetting that their yardstick of assessment was often attendance by the whole community. Evidence assembled more recently shows that Scottish cities commonly enjoyed higher rates of attendance in 1851 than their rural hinterlands. Thus, for example, Edinburgh had 63 attenders per 100 in the population whereas the surrounding rural areas of Midlothian had only 45.[16] Part of the explanation lies in the fact that urban areas, unlike the countryside, were served, among Presbyterians, not just by the Church of Scotland and the Free

Church, but also by the United Presbyterians. In the cities there was a large, more populist denomination competing successfully for souls. Again buildings were important. As in the Highlands, so in the burgeoning towns there were inadequate facilities for worship in the early nineteenth century. The 1840s, however, brought significant change. In Lanarkshire between 1841 and 1851 the number of church sittings went up from 232 per 1,000 to 302 per 1,000.[17] Special efforts followed in the cities. It became a standard feature of a middle-class congregation to have one or more attached mission causes in deprived areas.

Undenominational effort was also more marked in urban areas. In 1826 David Nasmith had founded the first City Mission in Glasgow, and by the end of the century his organisation had been widely copied. Even in the small town of Kilsyth, an undenominational mission could make a significant impact: founded in 1896, within only four years it had achieved attendances on Saturday evening of 150 and on Sunday evening of 200.[18] The visit of the American evangelists Dwight L. Moody and Ira D. Sankey in 1873 gave fresh impetus to urban mission, especially in Glasgow, where, as a result, the United Evangelistic Association was created in 1874, the Tent Hall erected on Glasgow Green to seat 2,200 in 1876 and the Bible Training Institute established to train evangelists in 1892. The gospel seized the imagination of much of urban Scotland.

The working classes
Even industrial workers were affected. A. A. MacLaren's *Religion and Social Class* (1974), a ground-breaking study of Aberdeen, contended that the working classes were absent from the churches in the mid-nineteenth century. Offering a Marxist analysis, MacLaren argued that church discipline amounted to an attempt at social control by the middle classes. The resentment of the working classes kept them away from worship.[19] MacLaren's influential interpretation, however, has subsequently been overturned by evidence from elsewhere. Peter Hillis has shown from a sample of Glasgow congregations that in the period 1845-1865, 75% of members of the Church of Scotland and 54%

of non-established Presbyterians were working-class. The element of truth in the earlier view is that *unskilled* workers and their families, the poorest strata of society, were indeed largely absent from worship. Of the working-class church-goers examined by Hillis, 69% from the Church of Scotland and as many as 80% from non-established Presbyterian churches belonged to families where there was a skill.[20] Analysis of other places has confirmed Hillis's findings: the working classes were not beyond the pale of the churches; but worshippers were largely drawn from the artisan class, those possessing skills and respectability.

This phenomenon was partly a result of the influence of businessmen, who sometimes encouraged churchgoing by their example, their expectations and prospects of promotion. In Dundee, for example, the Lochee United Presbyterian congregation benefited in this way from the support of members of the Cox family, owners of the largest firm of jute manufacturers in the world.[21] A potent bond with the working classes of all grades, furthermore, consisted of the rites of passage conducted under church auspices: baptisms, weddings and funerals. These occasions entailed regular contact even with the families of the poor at a time when children were numerous and infant mortality high. MacLaren discovered that in Aberdeen, although only 39% of the population attended church, fully 92% of the population a few years earlier had possessed some 'church connection' formed by contacts of this kind.[22] The evidence now suggests that industrial workers formed another substantial success story.

Male membership of churches
Nor should it be supposed that men in general were beyond the range of the gospel. The relation of churchgoing to gender has been much less investigated than its relation to class. We know that on the continent it was often the case that very few men attended worship. In two French Roman Catholic dioceses at the start of the twentieth century, for instance, there were five female communicants for every one male.[23] In England the standard ratio for Nonconformist membership during the late nineteenth century was around two women for every man.[24] Scotland seems to have

fared rather better in the evangelisation of men. Of the founding members of Coatbridge Relief Church in 1837, for example, twenty-four were women but forty-one men.[25] It could be pointed out, however, that Coatbridge was then a place where frontier conditions prevailed. The new ironworks were drawing in men, but there was still a paucity of women. Recent research nevertheless shows that in the much more settled conditions of Stirling the ratio approximated to one woman for each man on the communion roll at the end of the century. In one large Church of Scotland congregation there were actually more male than female members, a most unusual phenomenon in European perspective.[26]

The reasons are still largely speculative. Perhaps the practice of family worship encouraged male participation; but that factor should have operated equally in English Nonconformity. Perhaps the dominance of Presbyterianism in the community made male membership more a matter of social expectation. Certainly the eldership, then confined to men, was revived under Chalmers' influence in the earlier part of the century, so providing role models of lay involvement in church affairs.[27] In any case it is becoming clear that the churches managed to draw men into their membership.

Women in the churches

Women, however, were far from being left out. They were drawn to church by a quest for sociability. There was frequently no alternative focus for women in the community, for the bar was not for the respectable. Hence there arose a plethora of women's meetings, clothing societies, sewing circles and mothers' meetings that provided female companionship. The Church of Scotland began to institutionalise these gatherings with the Woman's Guild, designed for those in 'practical Christian work', from 1887.[28] Since we cannot make a window into people's souls, it is difficult to estimate the relative commitment of the sexes, but the evidence of church activities suggests that in general women identified more closely with the life of their congregations.

In Victorian churches the bulk of the work was performed by women. They took paid engagement as cleaners, door openers and area missionaries. Increasingly over time Sunday school teaching was in female hands. Whereas in the 1850s some two-thirds of Sunday school teachers in Scotland were male, by the 1890s the majority was female.[29] Women dominated fund-raising, whether through permanent committees or through *ad hoc* bazaars. Crucially, they were responsible for the bulk of house-to-house visitation. Lady visitors undertook the work alongside the minister, and few other men, certainly after the 1860s, joined in. The primary purpose of visitation was spiritual, to enquire into the religious well-being of each family, but it was also financial, for the visitors often acted as collectors of the main church giving.[30] It seems clear that the home missionary and money-raising roles of the churches both depended overwhelmingly on women.

Yet leadership rarely came to them. The Central Committee of the Church of Scotland's Woman's Guild itself was not chaired by a woman until as late as 1935.[31] There was, it is true, a significant number of female preachers in the revival atmosphere of the 1860s, especially among the emerging Brethren.[32] After 1888, when the Church of Scotland first appointed them, deaconesses in several denominations were put in charge of mission districts and so performed virtually the same duties as ministers. But these are the exceptions. In general the work was done by women; the leadership was supplied by men. The female mobilisation was substantially responsible for the impact of the churches.

Work among children
Children were by no means neglected in the home missionary strategy. Traditional Sabbath catechising continued, especially in the north. New ventures were launched such as the Children's Special Services Mission, which first appeared in Scotland in 1877 and was soon to be found organising month-long beach missions.[33] Sunday schools, however, were the main agency. Often originally a civic effort, as in Glasgow, Sunday schools had become attached to particular congregations by the 1840s. They enjoyed an astonishing degree of success. In Glasgow at about their peak, in 1891, 60% of the children aged five to fifteen were enrolled in a

Sunday school, and of them perhaps 75% attended on any given day. Thus nearly half Glasgow's relevant age-group were in attendance each Sunday.[34] Day schools were often barely less religious in their curriculum at mid-century. Nor was there a drastic secularisation of public education. In England the 1870 Education Act prohibited denominational teaching, permitting basic Bible instruction only. In Scotland, by contrast, the 1872 Education Act allowed school boards to provide religious instruction according to 'use and wont'. That phrase meant in most places that the evangelical teaching common to the Reformed churches continued to be transmitted in state-sponsored education. This difference in pedagogic practice north and south of the border may well largely account for the higher degree of religious knowledge among Scottish troops than among English soldiers during the First World War.[35] Certainly the basic doctrinal understanding of the mass of the population was a huge advantage for the evangelist. Children were being prepared to receive the gospel.

The use of literature
Literature also goes some way towards explaining the evangelistic achievement of the Victorian period. In 1861 the National Bible Society of Scotland consolidated the former separate Edinburgh, Glasgow and local Bible societies. Shortly afterwards it was employing seventy Bible women in Edinburgh and Glasgow simply to sell Bibles and Testaments.[36] Much of the periodical publication around mid-century was religious. Perhaps best known was *Good Words*, the monthly general interest magazine with a Christian slant begun in 1860 by Norman MacLeod, the grandfather of George MacLeod. Denominational magazines flourished: *Life and Work*, the journal of the Church of Scotland, enjoyed a circulation of 81,000 only a year after its foundation in 1880.[37] A weekly newspaper packed with ecclesiastical news, *The British Weekly,* was edited from 1886 by William Robertson Nicoll, an enterprising Free Church minister turned journalist. These periodicals, it might be said, merely tended to reinforce Christian opinions: they were not evangelistic. Tracts, however, were. Peter Drummond, a Stirling seedsman, issued his first tract

in 1848, and over the next twenty-four years he despatched a staggering sixty million items.[38] Peter's nephew, the celebrated evangelist Henry Drummond, was one of those whose longer evangelistic works achieved a high circulation. His exposition of 1 Corinthians 13, *The Greatest Thing in the World* (1890), is still in print. The written word was a major medium for the gospel.

Territorial schemes

Territorial schemes were a form of systematic evangelism that deserve particular mention. The idea was the brainchild of Thomas Chalmers, a hugely influential figure over patterns of mission throughout the English-speaking world. In St John's Parish, Glasgow, from 1819 he allocated to each section an elder to co-ordinate, a deacon to provide poor relief and a missionary to visit. After the Disruption, recognising the need for denominational co-operation, he urged the Protestant bodies to divide up the cities for house-to-house visitation supplemented by schools, savings banks, reading rooms, cookery classes, laundry facilities and employment exchanges – an approximation to holistic mission. The grand aim was to reinforce religious practice with respectability, that supreme Victorian value, through self-reliance. Hence after a while every external agency was to withdraw, leaving a new working-class congregation to organise its own 'self-extension'.

In the earlier period after Chalmers' death in 1847, his own Free Church promoted the method, and when it fell into disfavour there during the 1870s, the Church of Scotland took it up because its essentials tallied closely with its parochial ideal.[39] Yet the method was also operated by the voluntaryists who rejected the parish system. From 1847, for instance, Coatbridge Relief Church staked out an area in which it ran fortnightly home meetings in various neighbourhoods, regular Sunday evening meetings, a Bible class and several Sunday schools – all under the care of a single missionary, Robert Barnes, who paid some 2,000 home visits a year. We do not know how many joined in his evening service because he refused to count attenders on the ground that it was sinful to number the Lord's people. But we know that his efforts were rewarded, because a separate branch church, working-class in ethos, was eventually set up in 1878.[40] Such systematic missionary activity bore fruit.

Philanthropy

Philanthropy was a dimension of territorial schemes but it was also much more widespread. In the nineteenth century there was no principled exclusion of social work from the Christian programme of the kind that emerged among conservative evangelicals in the twentieth. Thus free breakfasts were served to the destitute on Sunday mornings in the Tent Hall—about a thousand each week by the 1890s.[41] William Quarrier, a Baptist businessman. established his well known orphanage at Bridge of Weir in 1878.[42] The Church of Scotland Woman's Guild began a hospital in 1891, only four years after its launch.[43] The temperance movement too sponsored a great deal of social work. The churches took up the total abstinence campaign with gusto from the 1870s because they recognised drink as a serious obstacle to the gospel. Bands of Hope, designed to warn children against the dangers of alcohol, became common on church premises. By 1908 there were 147,000 members in Scotland.[44] The temperance movement, however, was responsible for a variety of popular 'counter-attractions' to the public house ranging from coffee bars to country excursions. Social benefits of many kinds drew people to church-related organisations and sometimes even to church membership.

Revival

A further reason for church growth, however, was revival. Traditionally associated with Presbyterian long communion seasons, revivals could still be provoked by these soul-searching experiences in the middle years of the century. There was one such at Kilsyth, for example, in 1839. By 1866, however, the next revival impulse in the town affected all the evangelical denominations, and that became the normal pattern.[45] The greatest wave of revival began in 1859. From August of that year, for instance, the Seamen's Chapel at Greenock was open every night and after six months at least 1,000 people had professed conversion.[46] Lanarkshire was also swept by revival, particularly among the miners, and as a result at least twelve Brethren assemblies were set up in the county during the 1860s.[47] A more planned variety of revival, however, had already made its appearance. Its chief source was the American evangelist Charles Finney, who believed that techniques such as the 'anxious seat' for awakened sinners could be deployed to maximise conversions. His methods were adopted by James Morison,[48] whose Evangelical Union came into being to put them into practice, and they made headway among the Baptists and the United Presbyterians.

An even greater change was associated with Moody, whose mission in Glasgow in the spring of 1873 demanded four addresses from him each day. Moody insisted on interdenominational co-operation and introduced fresh techniques such as enquiry rooms.[49] Thereafter revival became a synonym for a special mission, with rather dubious results in some cases. In 1894, for example, the Kilsyth Methodists ran a six-week mission at the end of which the entire Sunday school of over three hundred children rose to 'decide for Christ'.[50] Many were probably playing follow my leader; yet no doubt some of the conversions were genuine. Revivalism became less a spontaneous than a contrived matter as Victoria's reign wore on, but it did still spread the gospel. Thus a whole catalogue of reasons explains why evangelical Christianity advanced in Victorian Scotland.

Post-Victorian Scotland

We can now turn to the post-Victorian period, though several of the developments to be surveyed were already emerging before 1901. Again, before considering the strategies of the churches it is helpful to look at the obstacles. None of the problems that had inhibited the progress of the faith in the nineteenth century had disappeared, but each of them had grown less acute with the passing of time. Poverty survived, but the greater wealth of society at large had percolated through even to the poor. Drink still kept people away from church, but public houses were under more restrictions. Popular culture remained resistant to the preaching of the gospel, but society at large was permeated by Christian assumptions, especially about the centrality of family life. So the difficulties inherited from the past were, if anything, rather easier to overcome. Yet there was a range of fresh obstacles, and they proved extremely difficult to surmount.

Suburbanisation

One was the redistribution of population by suburbanisation. As early as the 1830s, a suburb designed for the upper middle classes had begun to rise on the western outskirts of Glasgow at Kelvinside. With the building of railways and the increasing prosperity of the times, it became possible from the 1870s for the lower middle classes and even some of the upper working classes to join the flight from the dirt and smell of the city centres. By 1900 the pattern of house occupation that was to dominate the whole twentieth century had come into existence. Different areas were occupied by different social classes. The creation of state-subsidised housing after the First World War simply accentuated the tendency. Consequently middle-class leaders deserted the city-centre churches as they moved to the suburbs.[51] In some cases inner-city congregations tried to struggle on, depleted in resources both human and material; in other cases they gave up the unequal contest and closed down. Meanwhile in the comfortable areas on the fringe of the cities, the middle classes lived apart from the working classes and rapidly became unaccustomed to home missionary work among them. Suburbs created barriers between the churched and the unchurched.

Class consciousness

A related problem was the rise of class consciousness. When people live apart, they think apart. Class consciousness had not been deeply rooted among the working people during most of the nineteenth century, but from the 1880s new voices could be heard calling for solidarity in the pursuit of their common interests against the capitalists. Prominent among them was Keir Hardie, soon the leader of the Independent Labour Party. In 1899 he attacked Lord

Overtoun, a leading elder in the Free Church and president of the Glasgow United Evangelistic Association, for the treatment of the workers at his Shawfields chemical works. They were paid a pittance for twelve hours' work a day with no time off for meals; the works had poor sanitary conditions; the manufacture of chrome caused abscesses; and, most damaging of all in the light of the proprietor's evangelical allegiance, many of his employees had to work on the Sabbath. Overtoun was being indicted for hypocrisy and could only reply rather lamely that he was unaware of these circumstances.[52] The episode was a symptom and also a precipitant of the growing willingness to reject deference to businessmen and to scorn their Christian profession. Rising class consciousness, especially in the cities, created a fresh hostility to religion.

Welfare reforms

From its first decade the twentieth century saw a steady increase in the provision of public welfare. The pre-war Liberal welfare reforms, including unemployment benefit and old age pensions, were laying the foundations of the welfare state. Those in need no longer turned first to the churches for philanthropic support. Although the extent of the benefits was still relatively meagre in the 1930s, one of the traditional ways in which the churches had maintained friendly contact with the poor was largely supplanted.

Public leisure facilities

Moreover, forms of popular recreation multiplied. A higher standard of living for the working classes meant the expansion of commercial facilities to cater for their taste in leisure. Music halls sprang up from the 1870s, picture palaces from the 1910s, radio from the 1920s. Perhaps most serious of all, there was a mushrooming of organised sport, and in particular football. Although matches were rarely if ever played on Sundays, men and boys found their primary social outlet through joining or (more often) watching sport. A new and powerful alternative to church-based activities had arisen.

The churches' response to change

How did the churches respond to these new developments? Part of the answer is that they continued the methods of the Victorian years, whether distributing tracts or organising meetings for women. The techniques had succeeded in the past and so there was a natural reluctance to modify them. Nor was that always a foolish policy, for in many areas circumstances had barely altered at all. Along the Moray Firth coast, for example, there was in 1921 a revival among the fishermen associated with the evangelist Jock Troup that exactly reproduced scenes remembered by the elderly from 1859.[53] Yet there were also attempts to grapple with the new patterns of twentieth-century life.

'Opportunities for harmless pleasure'

There were efforts by the churches, in the first place, to enter the field of leisure. Since entertainments were available outside the places of worship, it was calculated, then if the worshipping communities were to retain the loyalty of their young people, they must provide comparable attractions. The church was right, commented *Life and Work* in 1922, to supply under her own aegis 'opportunities for harmless pleasure'.[54] Especially in the wake of the First World War, when the needs of the returning servicemen were to the fore in everybody's mind, there were efforts to organise such games as billiards, tennis and football. Perhaps less was done by Protestants than by Roman Catholics; and probably less was offered than in England, and much less than in the United States. Yet there was a serious attempt to retain a bridge to the uncommitted through leisure facilities.

A social gospel

The social gospel should be seen as an equivalent means of retaining contact with the masses of the population. Often this phase of recent history is recalled as a divergence from the true gospel, but it was neither originally nor mainly so. Dr David Watson, perhaps the chief protagonist of the social gospel in the Church of Scotland, who urged that there must be a Christianisation of the industrial system, nevertheless insisted that the primary duty of the church is the regeneration of men. 'Until men realise the kingdom of God within them', he argued, 'they will never construct it in the world.'[55] So the social gospel should be recognised as an attempt by evangelicals to respond to the trends of the times, in particular the aspiration of the class-conscious workers for a better society. Watson managed to prompt his General Assembly to establish a Church of Scotland Committee on Social Work in 1904, beginning its many operations with a Labour Home for Destitute Men in Edinburgh.[56] The United Free Church was slower off the mark, but appointed a Special Committee on Social Problems in 1909.[57] Much of the activity stimulated by the social gospel was channelled into the temperance cause, since total abstinence was widely seen as the key to the social problem. Consequently there was extensive church involvement in the plebiscites about a local veto on the sale of alcohol that began in 1920. In that year, for instance, James Barr was given leave of absence from the ministry of the United Free Church to engage in the 'no licence' campaign, his first step towards becoming a Member of Parliament.[58] The social gospel was the rationale for a large part of mission in the inter-war years.

Anti-Catholicism
Another strategy that found favour in this period was founded on anti-Catholicism. Outbursts of anti-Catholic feeling had peppered the nineteenth century, but it found fresh favour during the high unemployment of the decades following the First World War. Job rivalry with Roman Catholics became more intense and, at the same time, there was resentment that the 1918 Education Act had made Roman Catholic schools chargeable to the rates. At the 1936 municipal election in Edinburgh a Protestant Action party under John Cormack gathered 31% of the vote.[59] During the First World War *Life and Work* had described the Roman Catholic Church as an enemy of Britain, and in its wake John White, the dominant voice in the counsels of the Church of Scotland, called for the repatriation of Irish immigrants to Scotland.[60] To many evangelicals it seemed a sensible preliminary to effective mission to remove the impervious Catholics from the land.

A secularised church

A problem common to all three twentieth-century approaches reviewed so far is that they were counter-productive. The investment of limited resources in social, and even political, enterprises meant that they were transferred away from the more strictly religious sphere. Here was the basis for the conservative evangelical disquiet with the social gospel that began to gather force at the same period. Even *Life and Work* became worried by 1930 that organising sports was yet another burden for the hard-pressed minister and cautiously suggested that the question of activities not directly relevant to the church's purpose needed thinking out.[61] Far from sacralising society, most of these methods were secularising the church. Moreover they were alienating those who enjoyed an occasional drink, together with the whole of the nominally Catholic community, from the message of the gospel. The flawed nature of these strategies helps explain the falling membership in relation to population that became apparent after about 1905.

Innovations in mission

Yet there were other techniques of mission in these years. With the consolidation of most Presbyterians into the reconstituted Church of Scotland in 1929, there was a renewed emphasis on church order and parish structure. In 1925 the General Assembly had set apart six missioners for special evangelistic work within the church.[62] Following reunion, a Forward Movement was planned. There was a call for service to the kingdom and in 1931 a special Glasgow Congress was frequently reminded that evangelism is the primary duty of the church.[63] Yet the emphasis in the Forward Movement was not on going beyond the bounds of ecclesiastical buildings to the unreached but on a deeper appreciation of their faith among existing church members.[64] No doubt some experienced a kindling of the spiritual life for the first time, but there can be no doubt that the normal Presbyterian approach was much less aggressive than in the Victorian years.

Para-church work also went forward. Young people were

mobilised by the Boys' Brigade, the Inter-Varsity Fellowship began to cater for students and bodies such as the Faith Mission sustained pioneer evangelism among adults. Perhaps most novel in this period was Frank Buchman's Oxford Group. Informal teams of 'life-changers' organised large-scale campaigns in which people were challenged to surrender to Christ. At the cell-like groups themselves there was much psychological jargon, together with explicit confession of wrongs. In this phase, the movement was substantially orthodox and incisively evangelistic. Its Edinburgh campaign of 1932 made a great stir.[65] There was therefore a counter-current of effective innovation in mission, but it was on a relatively small scale in comparison with the efforts of the previous century.

Conclusion

It has to be concluded that, as the statistics suggest, the churches were much less successful in the post-Victorian than in the Victorian epoch. Their smaller impact was a consequence both of greater obstacles and of less effective methods. Those may, in turn, be related to the milder preaching of the twentieth as against the nineteenth century, a theme that would need fuller analysis elsewhere. Yet even in the earlier twentieth century, evangelicalism in some form dominated the Scottish Protestant churches and their continuing proclamation still drew large numbers into Christian discipleship. Church adherence in the 1950s was, in absolute terms, barely less than it had been at its peak in the first decade of the century. Yet it is the Victorian period that stands out as a time of remarkable achievement in mission, an age of glory not of death. Evangelising, as it has been pointed out, did work.[66] Perhaps the record raises questions for a later time. Are Christians now as systematic in planning mission as was Thomas Chalmers? Are they as aware of the potential of Christian communications as was Peter Drummond? Do they look for God's generosity in spontaneous revival as much as the seamen of Greenock or the miners of Lanarkshire? Such questions are worth pondering as missionary strategies for the twenty-first century are up for consideration.

Notes

1. Thomas Rosie, *Statement and Appeal in Behalf of the Extension of Home Mission Agency to the Towns and Villages on the Coast from Montrose Northwards* (Aberdeen, 1858), p.7, quoted by Neil Dickson, 'Scottish Brethren: division and wholeness, 1838-1916,' in Harold H. Rowdon, ed., *Scottish Brethren 1838-1916 and Other Papers* (Exeter, 1990), p.9. This paper was delivered at the joint Evangelical Alliance/Scottish Evangelical Theology Society conference in September 1996 marking the 150th anniversary of the E.A.
2. Callum G. Brown, *The Social History of Religion in Scotland since 1730* (London, 1987), p.83.
3. Peter Brierley and Fergus Macdonald, *Prospects for Scotland 2000: Trends and Tables from the 1994 Scottish Church Census* (Edinburgh, 1995), p.16.
4. Brown, *Social History*, p.63.
5. Callum G. Brown, 'Religion, Class and Church Growth', in W. Hamish Fraser and R. J. Morris (eds), *People and Society in Scotland: II: 1830-1914* (Edinburgh, 1990), p.314.
6. Callum G. Brown, 'The Costs of Pew-Renting', *The Journal of Ecclesiastical History*, 38 (1987).
7. Daniel C. Paton, 'Drink and the Temperance Movement in Nineteenth-Century Scotland', unpublished Edinburgh Ph.D. thesis, 1977, pp.131-5.
8. *The Revival*, 25 February 1860, p.61.
9. Dickson, 'Scottish Brethren', p.18.
10. Sarah Williams, 'Urban Popular Religion and the Rites of Passage', in Hugh McLeod (ed.), *European Religion in the Age of Great Cities, 1830-1930* (London, 1995).
11. Edward Royle, *Victorian Infidels: The Origins of the British Secularist Movement, 1791-1866* (Manchester, 1974), p.237.
12. Brown, 'Religion, Class and Church Growth', p.313.
13. Donald E. Meek, 'Evangelical Missionaries in the Early Nineteenth-Century Highlands', *Scottish Studies*, 28 (1987).
14. Allan I. Macinnes, 'Evangelical Protestantism in the Nineteenth-Century Highlands', in Graham Walker and Tom Gallagher (eds), *Sermons and Battle Hymns: Protestant Popular Culture in Modern Scotland* (Edinburgh, 1990), p.62.
15. T. C. Smout, *A Century of the Scottish People, 1830-1950* (London, 1987 edn), chap. 8.
16. R. J. Morris, 'Urbanisation and Scotland', in Fraser and Morris (eds), *People and Society*, p.92.
17. Brown, 'Religion, Class and Church Growth', p.313.
18. James Hutchinson, *Weavers, Miners and the Open Book: A History of*

Kilsyth (Kilsyth, 1986), p.155. The congregation was to evolve into one of the earliest Pentecostal churches in Scotland.

19. A. A. MacLaren, *Religion and Social Class: The Disruption Years in Aberdeen* (London, 1974).

20. Peter Hillis, 'Presbyterianism and Social Class in Mid-Nineteenth-Century Glasgow: A Study of Nine Churches', *The Journal of Ecclesiastical History*, 32 (1981).

21. John Quinn, 'The Mission of the Churches to the Irish in Dundee, 1846-1886', unpublished Stirling M.Litt. thesis, 1993, p.237.

22. MacLaren, *Religion and Social Class,* pp.44,126.

23. Thomas Kselman, 'The Varieties of Religious Experience in Urban France', in McLeod (ed.), *European Religion*, p.168.

24. Clive D. Field, 'Adam and Eve: Gender in the English Free Church Constituency', *The Journal of Ecclesiastical History*,44 (1993).

25. William Hamilton, *Work and Prayer: The Story of a Church in an Industrial Community* (Coatbridge, 1937), p.59.

26. Linda Jeffrey, 'Women in the Churches of Nineteenth-Century Stirling', unpublished Stirling M.Litt. thesis, 1997.

27. G. D. Henderson, *The Scottish Ruling Elder* (London, 1935), pp.229-31.

28. Mamie Magnusson, *Out of Silence: The Woman's Guild, 1887-1987* (Edinburgh, 1987), p.55.

29. Callum G. Brown, 'The Sunday-School Movement in Scotland, 1780-1914', *Records of the Scottish Church History Society*, 21 (1981), p.19.

30. Jeffrey, 'Women in the Churches of Nineteenth-Century Stirling.'

31. Magnusson, *Out of Silence*, p.62.

32. Neil Dickson, 'Modern Prophetesses: Women Preachers in the Nineteenth-Century Scottish Brethren', *Records of the Scottish Church History Society*, 25 (1993).

33. Robert S. Hill, *The Sword Unsheathed: The Story of the Scripture Union in Scotland* (Glasgow, 1992), pp.14-16.

34. Brown, 'Sunday-School Movement', p.14.

35. *The Army and Religion* (London, 1919).

36. Fergus Macdonald, 'The Bible Societies in Scotland', in David F. Wright (ed.), *The Bible in Scottish Life and Literature* (Edinburgh, 1988), pp.35-6.

37. *Life and Work*, May 1912, pp.134-5.

38. N. M. de S. Cameron (ed.), *Dictionary of Scottish Church History and Theology* (Edinburgh, 1993), p.798.

39. Stewart J. Brown, 'Thomas Chalmers and the Communal Ideal in Victorian Scotland', in T. C. Smout (ed.), *Victorian Values* (Oxford, 1992).

40. Hamilton, *Work and Prayer*, pp.76-109.

41. F. V. Waddleton, 'The Bible Training Institute, Glasgow', unpublished typescript, 1979, p.10.
42. Alexander Gammie, *William Quarrier and the Story of the Orphan Homes of Scotland* (London, n.d.).
43. Magnusson, *Out of Silence*, p.69.
44. Cameron (ed.), *Dictionary,* p.816.
45. Hutchinson, *Weavers, Miners and the Open Book*, chap. 9, pp.73-5.
46. *The Revival*, 28 January 1860, p.30.
47. Dickson, 'Scottish Brethren', p.11.
48. Harry Escott, *A History of Scottish Congregationalism* (Glasgow, 1960), p.116.
49. James F. Findlay, *Dwight L. Moody: American Evangelist, 1837-1899* (Chicago, 1969), chap. 5.
50. Hutchinson, *Weavers, Miners and the Open Book*, p.118.
51. E.g. D. R. Watts, 'Glasgow and Dunbartonshire', in D.W. Bebbington (ed.), *The Baptists in Scotland: A History* (Glasgow, 1988), pp.167-71.
52. Donald Carswell, *Brother Scots* (London, 1927), pp.206-9.
53. Stanley C. Griffin, *A Forgotten Revival: East Anglia and N.E. Scotland – 1921* (Bromley, Kent, 1992), chap. 6.
54. *Life and Work*, March 1922, p.52.
55. *Life and Work*, October 1922, p.227.
56. Lewis L. L. Cameron, *The Challenge of Need: A History of Social Service by the Church of Scotland, 1869-1969* (Edinburgh, 1971), p.24.
57. Donald J. Withrington, 'Non-Church-going, Church Organisation and "Crisis in the Church", c. 1880-c.1920', *Records of the Scottish Church History Society*, 24 (1991), p.217.
58. *The British Weekly*, 25 March 1920, p.566.
59. Cameron (ed.), *Dictionary*, p.211.
60. *Life and Work*, June 1918, p.85. Stewart J. Brown, ' "Outside the Covenant": the Scottish Presbyterian Churches and Irish Immigration, 1922-1938', *The Innes Review*, 42 (1991).
61. *Life and Work*, June 1930, p.251.
62. *Life and Work*, July 1925, p.147.
63. *Life and Work*, January 1931, p.17; December 1931, p.498.
64. *Life and Work*, March 1932, p.117.
65. D. W. Bebbington, 'The Oxford Group between the Wars', in W. J. Sheils and D. Wood (eds), *Voluntary Religion* (Studies in Church History, Vol.23) (Oxford, 1986).
66. Brown, 'Religion, Class and Church Growth', p.329.

Chapter 3

A Tale of Two Paradigms:
Mission in Scotland from 1946

William Storrar

1996 was a significant anniversary year to reflect on the history
of mission in Scotland. Not only was it the 150th anniversary of
the founding of the Evangelical Alliance, with the prominent
support of leading Scottish evangelicals like Thomas Chalmers,
an early 19th century pioneer of urban mission in Scotland. It was
also the 200th anniversary of the famous debate on foreign
missions held in the General Assembly of the Church of Scotland
in 1796. This led eventually to overseas mission work by the church
itself rather than by voluntary missionary societies. The Church
of Scotland's work in India was pioneered by Alexander Duff,
who went on to become the first college professor of missiology
in the world, in the chair of Evangelistic Theology at New College
and the Glasgow and Aberdeen Free Church Colleges. And 1996
was also the 50th anniversary of the death in 1946 of one of
Scotland's few theologians of mission in the 20th century,
Professor David Cairns Sr., who taught at Christ's College,
Aberdeen. Cairns was chairman of one of the key commissions
and editor of probably the finest report produced for the 1910
Edinburgh World Missionary Conference, on relations with other
religions. He also contributed several substantial articles on
mission to the International Review of Mission. As someone who
was then teaching courses on mission at Aberdeen University, it
was therefore a particular honour to stand in that Scottish Reformed
and Evangelical tradition of missiology and reflect on the more
recent history of mission in Scotland at the 1996 SETS and EA
conference. This essay develops themes first presented in a paper
given at that conference, on such an auspicious anniversary

occasion; with the added pleasure now of honouring such a distinguished and scholarly friend of mission in Scotland, Dr Geoffrey Grogan.

I wish to offer not a detailed history of mission in Scotland from 1946 to the present but some preliminary missiological reflections on that history; with a view to asking what the churches and Christians need to learn from that recent history for the fresh work of mission in the millennium. As my opening comments on the three 1996 anniversaries indicate, modern Scottish mission history cannot be understood except in terms of its active engagement in the wider British and international debates and movements in mission theology and practice. Mission in Scotland from 1946 to the present must be seen at the outset, therefore, within a wider understanding of the history of modern mission in the West. I wish to do so from the perspective of the late South African missiologist,David Bosch, whose thesis concerns the nature of mission in the 20th century.

The Modern Paradigm of Mission

In his magisterial study of the history and theology of Christian mission over 2000 years, *Transforming Mission*, Bosch argues that each major era in the history of the Christian church has operated with an overarching and accompanying missiological paradigm; each with its different and distinct set of ruling biblical, theological and cultural assumptions and motifs concerning the nature of the Gospel and its witness and work in the world. So he writes of the missionary paradigms of the early church, the Eastern church, the medieval Roman Catholic Church and the Protestant Reformation. In particular, Bosch describes Protestant and Evangelical missions from the later 18th century onwards as operating within what he calls the modern paradigm of mission ' in the wake of the Enlightenment'; reflecting not only biblical convictions about the Great Commission and later the social gospel, but also understanding the Christian mission which followed on from these biblical motifs in terms of the Enlightenment's belief in progress, voluntary action, pragmatism and the universal claims of Western civilization. Therefore the modern era in mission saw not only an extraordinary missionary spread of Christianity in the non-Western world, but also the linking of Western mission and indeed Protestant Christianity as a whole with Western culture, imperialism and religious divisions. Partly under the impact of critical thought and class conflict on the churches in the 19th and earlier 20th centuries, the modern paradigm also operated latterly with a damaging split between an understanding of mission as saving souls and a view of mission as social action. Above all, mission was understood in terms of what some in the churches and particular church or voluntary agencies did in mission work; especially among 'the heathen' abroad or among the unchurched poor at home, and through specific evangelistic or socially improving activities.

The Modern Crisis of Mission: the Crisis of Modernity
Bosch sees the Edinburgh 1910 conference as the final flowering of that self-confident Western approach to world mission: 'Edinburgh represented the all-time high-water mark in Western missionary enthusiasm, the zenith of the optimistic and pragmatic approach to missions' – evangelizing the world in this generation.[1] However, the 20th century which the Edinburgh 1910 conference thought would see the final triumph and dominance of Christianity around the globe, linked to the civilising impact of scientific progress, has turned out very differently for the Western churches. Bosch characterises it as a century of crisis for the modern, Enlightenment paradigm of mission. The non-Western churches have asserted their independence and indigenous, locally contextualized Christianity, and grown to the extent that they now form the majority of the world's Christians; while the mainstream Western churches have had to come to terms with their own institutional decline and the secularization, indifference and even hostility of their own Western society.

Even more fundamentally, this has been a century of crisis for the Enlightenment world of modernity itself, Bosch argues (along with many commentators). After two world wars, the Holocaust and Hiroshima, and with the worsening ecological crisis, the collapse of communism in the West, resurgent nationalisms and fundamentalist religions, the deepening poverty, debt, ill-health and internal chaos of many Third World countries (with women and children the poorest and most vulnerable), the proliferation of vicious local and ethnic wars (now into Europe itself), the chemical slavery imposed by the illegal drug trade on millions of all social classes, and the globalization of the world economy, so the 'old' assumptions of the modern world no longer apply. Modernity's confidence in science and critical reason to deliver unalloyed progress and universal prosperity, its related split between fact and value, its material base in the industrial manufacturing economy of mass production and lifelong (male) full employment, and related culture of nuclear families, mass entertainment and mass-membership institutions, have all been swept away or brought seriously into question by the lived experience and structural changes of the 20th century.

In its closing decades, we have witnessed the rise of the post-industrial, knowledge-based economy with its constantly innovating computing and information technologies. It operates through global corporations and financial markets, but has regional centres of entrepreneurial research and development. It offers short-term contracts and low wages for the ageing many, but high educational attainments and monetary rewards for the young employed few. It is driven by a culture of consumerism, risk and insecurity, and is distinguished, above all, from earlier periods by the sheer rapidity and relentlessness of change in every area of life. Even the political order of modernity, with its sovereign nation-states, has found itself increasingly powerless against such global economic forces. At the same time centralised states like the United Kingdom are having to devolve or hand over power to internal national and external international levels of government, like the Scottish Parliament and the European Union. Along with these global patterns, there is also an assertion of individual autonomy and choice in the 'pick and mix' culture of shopping, leisure and media; an affirmation of local and multicultural identities, human rights and gender equality; a suspicion of the universal claims of religion and ideology, science and progress, expert opinion and institutional authority; and a reaffirmation of a holistic, even spiritual, understanding of human life and all life on this fragile planet.

Sociologists debate how these undoubted socio-economic, cultural and political changes should be interpreted and labelled: whether as the advanced stages of 'late modernity'; the end of the 'simple modernity' of the Enlightenment and first industrial revolution and the advent of a second, more self-aware and self-critical, 'reflexive or second modernity'; or even as the emergence of a 'postmodern' world. For Bosch, the later 20th century has been witnessing the emergence of that 'postmodernity', a social world significantly and fundamentally different from the world of modernity, at once liberating and fragmenting, empowering and marginalising for the world's populations. In a related way, the churches were also witnessing, through a mid-20th century sense of crisis about the legitimacy and purpose of mission, the decline of their own once dominant modern Enlightenment paradigm of mission and its slow, uneven replacement with the new cultural assumptions and theological motifs of what Bosch termed the 'postmodern paradigm'.

The Postmodern Paradigm of Mission

As evidence of this emerging postmodern paradigm of mission, Bosch documented the converging understanding of mission evident across the ancient and modern ecclesial and theological divides of Christendom, in Catholic, Orthodox, Protestant (Ecumenical), Evangelical, and Pentecostal traditions. He argued that many biblical and theological elements of mission which had been split asunder or lost sight of in the modern era were being reunited and recovered. For Bosch, the Lausanne Covenant and its later conferences and documents are evidence of that convergence in the evangelical movement, with their affirmation of evangelism and social concern in mission. In this ecumenical paradigm (ecumenical in this specific sense of converging missiological views across the traditions), mission is understood primarily as God's mission, the *missio Dei*, and not primarily as the church's mission: God the Father sending God's Son into the world, in the power of the Spirit, and with the incarnate, crucified, risen and ascended Son, sending God's Spirit on the church, in order to send it out into all the world, as a witness in word and action to God's coming Kingdom in the world. In this paradigm, mission becomes for the church a participation in God's triune and continuing mission in the world, and not primarily what the church does in, for example, evangelism and social concern or the earlier 'foreign and home missions'.

Seen from this perspective, every aspect of the church's life is a participation in God's mission. Mission in the postmodern paradigm is not restricted to certain Christians or activities labelled missionary or evangelistic. The whole church, especially the local congregation, is defined as the 'church-in-mission', the missionary community; and committed to its unity-in-mission with partner churches rather than to denominational rivalry. Activities which in the modern paradigm were seen as either the whole of mission or competing priorities, are now seen as complementary dimensions of the one, larger, multidimensional and holistic mission. In particular, evangelism is seen as the non-coercive invitation to personal faith in Jesus Christ as Saviour and Lord; cross-cultural mission is practised as a faithful witness to the unique claims of Christ in non-aggressive dialogue with neighbours of other living faiths and of no formal religion; and social action is understood as the confronting of structural sin and the transforming of society through the liberating Gospel of the Kingdom. These are all affirmed in the postmodern paradigm as integral and essential dimensions of the one mission of God.

Core activities of the Church, like worship and ministry, are also understood as forms of participation in the *missio Dei*; and for all God's people, not just those in ordained or commissioned ministries. Ministry too is always ministry-in-mission, just as authentic theology comes out of critical reflection on the theory and practice of mission in the contemporary world (as it has done since the New Testament documents). And all these dimensions of the one mission of God, including the transmission and proclamation of the Gospel and the obedient reading of Scripture, must be contextualized in each local and cultural situation. All Christians and congregations are called to mission in every aspect of their life and work. As the late Lesslie Newbigin taught us, the congregation itself is a hermeneutic of the Gospel in the midst of the world; in its common life in Christ and in its conviction that the Gospel is public truth. Sometimes the mission dimension will be implicit and at other times it will be made explicit and focal, but always it will be present, acknowledged and affirmed as a participation in Christ's mission, through the Spirit, and to God's glory.

All this is a long way from the image of mission 'in the wake of the Enlightenment', as the triumph of the Christian West through its heroic and select missionary band of evangelists, educators and medical workers. For Bosch, that Enlightenment paradigm and its exemplars are not to be despised but critically re-evaluated, then taken up and transformed in the emerging, post-Enlightenment patterns and models of mission. Over time, this will lead eventually to a whole new framework or paradigm of mission. Bosch suggests that the process of paradigm shift in the church takes many decades if not centuries, during which the once dominant and the now emerging paradigms will often co-exist, even in the same person's thinking and practice in mission. Indeed, the distinctive feature of mission at the end of the century is that sense of uncertainty which is characteristic of a period of paradigm shift. Scotland itself has been a major contributor to the modern paradigm, in both thinking and missionary personnel, as I have suggested in my introduction. But is there any evidence to suggest that the history of mission within Scotland in the second half of the 20th century shares in the crisis and decline of Bosch's modern paradigm and the emergence of an alternative postmodern theory and practice of mission? It is to that question that we can now turn, using the above missiological perspective as our interpretative horizon on the Scottish scene.

Mission Since 1946: A Tale of Two Paradigms?
The picture of mission that we find in the ten years from the end of the Second World is an ambiguous one, in the terms of Bosch's missiological analysis. On the one hand, we can find so many of the traits of modern mission in the impressive initiatives in

evangelism which are such a marked feature of Scottish church life from 1946-55. On the other hand, there are clear features of what Bosch would wish to call postmodern mission theology and practice present in that same postwar movement. No one typifies this creative tension between overlapping mission paradigms better than Tom Allan, the Church of Scotland minister who had remarkable outreach ministries in his North Kelvinside and St George's Tron parishes in Glasgow and was the organiser for the 'Tell Scotland' movement in the 1950s.

Clearly, Tom Allan was at the centre of a typically modern initiative in mass evangelism, the 1955 'All Scotland Crusade' with the American evangelist Billy Graham. During six weeks in the Kelvin Hall, Glasgow, in open air rallies and special relay meetings around Scotland. Tom Allan records that 'a total of 1,185,360 people in Scotland attended meetings of one kind or another directly connected with the Crusade'.[2] Mission was seen here as the activity of evangelism, certainly involving the laity as supporters and organisers, but relying on the gifts and role of specific evangelists and ministers, above all the electrifying persona of the young Billy Graham himself. Churches and congregations across the denominations worked together to support the Crusade and to receive the converts and enquirers, but again played a supportive rather than a primary role. While the attendances at the 1955 Crusade were impressive and many lives were changed, the long-term impact of such initiatives in mass event evangelism on the post-war life and mission of the church in Scotland remains a matter of debate and requires further research. In the decades that followed, similar but much smaller scale mass evangelism events have continued in Scotland; mainly relying on international evangelists like Leighton Ford in the 1960s, Luis Palau in the 1970s and 80s, and even the return to Scotland of Billy Graham himself in 1991 and his son Franklin in 1999. After 1955, such evangelistic work has been more typically initiated by Christians in the smaller independent and new evangelical churches, and by some but not all evangelicals in the mainstream denominations (William Still was a notable critic after his initial evangelistic work with Billy Graham in Aberdeen in the later 1940s). The kind of cross-denominational, pan-Scotland event like the first Billy Graham Crusade, with a lead coming from ministers in the majority Church of Scotland of the stature of Tom Allan, did not return after 1955, however.

Some would argue that the decision to invite Billy Graham to lead this mass evangelistic form of mission was exactly what polarised the indigenous and broad 'Tell Scotland' movement, which had allowed for a more inclusive range of local and theological emphases under a common mission banner; from the personal evangelistic work of a D. P. Thomson to the 'mission of friendship' approach pioneered by George MacLeod and the Iona Community. Certainly by the 1960s, more radical Christians were interpreting mission as social and political action to challenge local and Third World injustices, and there seemed to be a growing chasm with the 'evangelistic types', who emphasised individual sin and salvation and the priority of soul-winning in mission. All these post-war developments would conform to the pattern of Bosch's modern paradigm of mission. And yet that is not the whole picture, and it certainly was not the whole picture with Tom Allan himself.

In June, 1953, only two years before his involvement in the All Scotland Crusade, Tom Allan finished writing what was to become a post-war classic of mission theology and practice, *The Face of My Parish*. Drawing on his own Glasgow experience of parish mission in his North Kelvinside church, and thoughtful reading of continental and especially French Catholic and Reformed studies of mission in a secular Western society, Allan developed what can only be described as a brilliant anticipation of key elements in later, postmodern missiology. Central to his understanding of mission was the local congregation itself. It was the ordinary members of the local church who had to engage in mission alongside their neighbours in the local community. The role of the ordained ministry was to equip and enable the members to engage in that missionary encounter, through the experience of learning and worship in community, especially in the small group. As Allan himself describes the development of his own missiology during the course of his North Kelvinside ministry:

Gradually three principles became articulate for me, and I began to hold them with increasing conviction. The first is that the solution to the vast problem of communicating the gospel to the masses who live outside the sphere of Christian fellowship is inextricably bound up with the local church ñ that the key to evangelism lies in the parish. Secondly, that the Church can only fulfil its function, and penetrate the secular world when it is exhibiting the life of a genuine and dynamic Christian community ñ the koinonia of the New Testament. And thirdly, the place of the layman is decisive.[3]

Though he did not use the language of the *missio Dei*, Allan clearly understood mission theologically in these terms. Early in his book, he asks the searching and foundational question for Bosch's postmodern paradigm: 'If we believe that Christ is Lord not only of the Church but of the world, and that the Church is his Body, the agent and instrument of his redemptive purpose, where do we begin?' As his bibliography shows, Allan was deeply read in the kind of European theology and studies of ministry and mission which fostered such a trinitarian and yet also socially contextualized approach, from Bonhoeffer's *The Cost of Discipleship* to Jacques Ellul's *The Presence of the Kingdom*, and Abbé Michonneau's *Revolution in a City Parish*, a study of the evangelization of pagan France. This reflects an impressive commitment to serious theological reflection for a busy parish minister, later to be associated with the less nuanced and more trans-Atlantic preaching of Billy Graham. The North Kelvinside parish visitors that Allan trained went on to discover for themselves what Bonhoeffer and Ellul and Michonneau affirmed, that God was already at work in the lives of local people who were not hostile to their approach; least of all the many Roman Catholic neighbours they met. The real missiological challenge for Allan and North Kelvinside was the resistance of some of his own church members to such outreach and to the restructuring of internal church life and organisation required by Christ's call to be a missionary congregation in that parish, the whole 'church-in-mission' rather than the church in which some do mission on the side. All of these issues are central to the postmodern understanding and practice of mission, discerned by Allan and his post-war French mentors forty years before the publication of Bosch's seminal study of this trend, *Transforming Mission: Paradigm Shifts in Theology of Mission.*

While Tom Allan went on to have a rich and effective ministry on a wider national and international scale after North Kelvinside, it is perhaps here, in retrospect that he made his most lasting contribution to mission in post-war Scotland; in his affirmation and articulation of mission as the participation of the local congregation and ordinary members in Christ's mission in the local community, with the life together of the Christian community as the key 'hermeneutic of the Gospel' in that mission, to use Newbigin's phrase. We may describe Allan's ministry in both North Kelvinside and the All Scotland Crusade as 'a tale of two paradigms', but it is a mark of the man that this would also be true of mission in Scotland as a whole after 1946. On the one side we find the recurring tendency among Scottish Christians to define mission in the solitary terms of one dimension or approach to outreach: with an emphasis on evangelistic events, or expository preaching, or charismatic experience or social engagement, as competing alternatives which must be embraced to the exclusion of the others.

However, we can also discern a recurring and growing appreciation of Allan's insight that mission is to be affirmed as God's many-sided but inclusive mission in the wider world, into which the local congregation and its ordinary members are called to participate in fellowship, witness and service. More holistic, postmodern forms of mission theology and practice can be discerned in Scotland from the 1970s onwards: in, for example, the IVF and later UCCF encouragement of social involvement as well as evangelism by Christian students; the renewed emphasis in the SCM and Iona Community of the link between spirituality, prayer and politics; the move in the Church of Scotland, the Scottish Episcopal Church, the Roman Catholic and other Churches in the 1980s and 90s to develop and train missionary congregations and the laity as the primary agents of mission in Scotland; the development of certain urban Scottish Baptist churches to become more community-orientated in their buildings, programmes and outreach; the partnership of ministers and Christians across the inherited Evangelical-Social Gospel divides in developing appropriate forms of church and mission in urban communities of multiple deprivation; the growing influence and work of bodies like the Scottish Lausannne Committee, CARE, Tear Fund and Evangelical Alliance Scotland in encouraging Evangelical Christians to be socially engaged as well as evangelistically active in mission; the impact across the denominational spectrum of Scottish and international thinkers like John and Olive Drane or Bill Hybels on mission to the postmodern generation; and the growing ecumenical and evangelical cooperation in ACTS (Action for Churches Together in Scotland) in developing local models of partnership and unity in mission.

All this must be set, however, against the backdrop of an issue that Tom Allan and that first post-war generation of mission pioneers did not have to address, but which has become absolutely central to mission in Scotland since the late 1950s – the problem of the churches' own institutional decline and the rapid 'de-Christianization' of Scottish society at large.

The Mission Crisis in Scotland

I have written elsewhere about the history and nature of the Church of Scotland's institutional decline, and a social-historical analysis of the phenomenon across all the churches can be found in Callum Brown's work. The statistical data and analysis of the pattern of falling church attendance and membership can be found in the work of the late Peter Bisset on the Church of Scotland, and in two recent church census studies of all the churches carried out by the National Bible Society of Scotland in 1984 and 1994 (Brierley and MacDonald, 1985 and 1995). Overall, we can see a pattern of decline in church membership and attendance in the mainstream Protestant churches since the mid-1950s and in the Catholic church since the 1970s. Even the newer house and charismatic churches, and some congregations in the smaller denominations like the Baptish Union and the Scottish Episcopal Church, have experienced only very small levels of growth in terms of their absolute numbers and as a proportion of the total church membership or total population in Scotland. Increasingly denominations and local churches have become preoccupied by the problems and burdens of institutional decline, typified by inappropriate and costly buildings, insufficient funds, drops in recruitment to an increasingly overstretched ordained ministry and priesthood, or a lack of youth and active members. Even more significant for understanding the more recent history of mission in Scotland than these institutional indices of decline, the churches – their members, ministers and leaders – face an energy-sapping crisis of morale and confidence in a society that increasingly sees its organisation, message and ethic as irrelevant to their lives and needs. In a generation, from the 1950s to the 1990s, Scotland has moved rapidly from being a modern, Christian society to a postmodern, pluralist nation.

Three Theses for Missiological Recovery

What kind of crisis does this pattern of decline and cultural shift represent for the churches and for mission in Scotland? Drawing on Bosch's missiological thesis, I wish to argue that the crisis in mission is precisely one of a church and society caught up in a theological and cultural paradigm shift. Let me briefly identify three of my own theses about the nature of that crisis, and possible options for recovery of nerve in mission.

Thesis 1

First, the crisis is historically one of the Scottish churches' success, not its failure in mission. It was precisely the success of its evangelistic mission, and the growth in church membership, in the decade after the Second World War which so ill-prepared the churches for the shock of decline and the increasing indifference or hostility of society, especially the post-Sixties generations, to institutional religion. From interviews which I have conducted with Church of Scotland ministers who worked or trained in the 1950s, there was a certain triumphalist sense that the future was one of church expansion and the final Christianization of Scottish society. Church Extension charges in the new, post-war housing schemes were bursting at the seams with hundreds and thousands of children in their Sunday Schools, and growing adult memberships. Lay Christian organisations, conferences and initiatives like the Kirk Weeks were also flourishing in the Fifties. Historians like Callum Brown would point to a much longer-term pattern of church decline already underway in Scottish society since the later 19th century.[4] But in the 1950s it seemed that significant and growing numbers of Scots still valued church membership and had a sense of institutional belonging. The challenge was more to the depth and quality of their Christian faith and commitment; or so many thought.

With hindsight, this may have led too many in the churches to think of mission as an appeal to lapsed or lukewarm church members to return to the fold, rather than to see mission as a cross-cultural encounter with those increasingly unfamiliar with the Christian story, never mind the Christian church, or even a once-common Christian society. Recovery of nerve in mission requires a shift from that triumphalist and now nostalgic view of Scotland as a lapsed Christian nation, and a humble re-mapping of Scottish society as a pluralist community of diverse neighbours; open to friendship, dialogue and the witness of Christian lives and communities of spiritual faith, moral integrity and social compassion but not to 'crusades' and 'Christian commando raids' to re-take Scotland for the churches, as in the Fifties.

Thesis 2

This leads me on to my second thesis about the nature of the post-war crisis in mission. Sociologically, the crisis is primarily one taking place in society at large and not uniquely or narrowly in the churches. I have argued elsewhere that the Church of Scotland made a creative and fruitful accommodation with the culture of modernity from the mid-18th to the mid-20th centuries, becoming in many ways a typically modern institution, in its patterns of mission, organisation, ministry, church culture, theology and ethos. The crisis of institutional decline for the Church of Scotland is inseparable from the decline of the larger culture and economy of modernity in Scotland, of which the Kirk was so integrated and prominent a part. A similar analysis of cultural accommodation with modernity could be argued for many of the other Scottish churches in this same period, as David Bebbington has argued for the evangelical churches and movement. As the sociologist David McCrone has argued, Scotland in the later 20th century has become a leading-edge postmodern nation; with the decline and closure of its heavy industries and the growth of its post-industrial financial, electronics and service economy; its alienation from Westminster and the British nation-state and assertion of its own political autonomy and Scottish identity; and in the decline of its range of typically modern, mass-membership institutions, from the Co-operative movement to the churches themselves.

Younger Scots, under forty, are now typically postmodern in their valuing of personal autonomy, freedom to create their own multiple and changing sense of identity and lifestyle, and enjoyment of the global market in consumer choice, work, travel, leisure and media entertainment. In the midst of this local Scottish experience of what is a global pattern of postmodern change, already identified earlier in this essay in relation to Bosch's analysis, Scots have not become more secular and rationalist in their beliefs. Surveys and the whole range of holistic health and New Age practices to be found in the High Street and in the work place show the new phenomenon of what the English sociologist Grace Davie has called 'believing without belonging'.[5] The post-modern era remains a religious age with a high degree of interest in spirituality and ethical concern, alongside a powerful and dominant culture of consumerism and materialism. What postmodern people will not buy is the modern package of institutional Christianity and church membership as the way to explore and practice belief.

The problem for the churches is that the culture they married in order to engage in a successful mission to modern Scotland, the culture of modernity, has died on them. Too often those engaging in mission have acted like a grieving partner, offering the wider postmodern society pictures and images and institutional relics of a beloved culture and way of life that has long since declined in contemporary Scotland and disappeared from younger generation's experience altogether. The crisis in mission since the 1960s has been a sociological and psychological one of cultural loss and bereavement, rather than entirely a matter of internal reasons for decline (such as lack of commitment, failure in preaching, or poor leadership). The churches must acknowledge that cultural change from modern to postmodern Scotland and re-think not only their patterns of church life and mission but also their understanding and practice of the Gospel itself. This will involve them in a shared pastoral experience of institutional grieving and loss for their cultural partner of modernity and the cosy life they shared together in 'Christian Scotland'. This will have to happen before they are free to embrace the new culture of postmodernity, not uncritically, in pluralist Scotland.

Thesis 3

This leads on finally to my third thesis. Theologically, the crisis in mission which the Scottish churches and Christians face at the start of the 21st century is the hopeful one of new birth, not decline. As David Bosch has suggested, it is a healthy thing for the Church to be in crisis in its sense of mission. The danger comes when it is complacent about its own mission, as if that could be identified unequivocally and without shame as identical with the mission of God in the world. Some of the worst mission practice and most inadequate theologies of mission have operated when the Church confidently and uncritically identified the sword with the cross and the empire with the cause of Jesus Christ or modernity with the Gospel. Postmodern Scotland, and the world of the new millennium, represents a fresh challenge to the churches to re-think the theory and practice of mission in the critical light of the one mission of God to the world, revealed though Jesus Christ, and lived out in the Spirit. This will also call for a critical engagement with that postmodern culture, and the refounding of the church as a Gospel community for post-modern times.

Bibliography

Tom Allan, *The Face of My Parish,* (London, SCM, 1954).

Tom Allan, *Crusade in Scotland...Billy Graham* (London, Pickering and Inglis, 1955).

Peter Bisset, *The Kirk and her Scotland: the struggle for a Missionary Church* (Edinburgh, Handsel Press 1986).

Peter Brierley and Fergus MacDonald, eds., *Prospects for Scotland: From a Census of the Churches in 1984* (Edinburgh, National Bible Society of Scotland, 1985).

Peter Brierley and Fergus MacDonald, eds., *Prospects for Scotland 2000: Trends and Tables from the 1994 Scottish Church Census* (Edinburgh, National Bible Society of Scotland. 1995).

Callum Brown, *The Social History of Religion in Scotland Since 1707,* (London, Methuen, 1987).

Callum Brown, *Religion in Society in Scotland Since 1707* (Edinburgh, Edinburgh University Press, 1997).

David J. Bosch, *Transforming Mission: Paradigm Shifts In Theology of Mission* (Maryknoll, NY, Orbis, 1991).

Grace Davie, *Religion in Britain Since 1945,* (Oxford, Blackwell, 1994).

Lesslie Newbigin, *The Gospel in a Pluralist Society* (London, SPCK, 1989).

William Storrar, 'Understanding the Silent Disruption', in *The Future of the Kirk,* edited by D. A. S. Fergusson and D. W. D. Shaw, *Theology in Scotland Occasional Paper No.2,* St Andrews University, St Mary's College, 1997.

William Storrar, 'Civic Calvinism: Source of Reformed Vitality', in *Reformed Vitality,* edited by Donald A. Luidens *et al.,* (Lanham, MD, University Press of America, 1998).

Willaim Storrar, 'From Braveheart to faintheart: Worship and Culture in Postmodern Scotland', in Bryan Spinks and Iain Torrance, eds., *To Glorify God: Essays on Modern Reformed Liturgy,* (Edinburgh, T & T Clark, 1999).

Notes

[1] David J. Bosch, *Transforming Mission: Paradigm Shifts In Theology of Mission* (Orbis, Maryknoll, NY, 1991), p. 338.

[2] Tom Allen, *Crusade in Scotland...Billy Graham* (Pickering & Inglis, London,1955), p. 8.

[3] Tom Allen, *The Face of My Parish* (SCM, London,1954), p. 66.

[4] Callum Brown, *The Social History of Religion in Scotland Since 1707* (Methuen, London,1987); also *Religion in Society in Scotland Since 1707* (Edinburgh University Press, Edinburgh, 1997).

[5] Grace Davie, *Religion in Britain Since 1945* (Blackwell, Oxford, 1945).

Chapter 4

Communicating the Gospel in Scotland Today

Peter Neilson

A quick tour of a map of Scotland highlights the variety of this land we call Scotland. From the Isle of Lewis to the housing schemes of Drumchapel, and from the linked parishes of the Borders to the city centre ministries in Edinburgh, the situations are very different. As the contexts vary so do the patterns of communicating the Gospel. For some it means street work among young people with alcohol problems, for others it means Alpha groups in the local hotel. For some it means training ten preachers and worship leaders to sustain worship in rural congregations. For others it means sitting for long hours with battered women to find images of God that help them draw near enough to let God heal their hurts.

Communicating the Gospel in Scotland today calls for courage and compassion, inventiveness and imagination. And it is happening! According to Dr James Engel,[1] communication involves a process in which the 'audience is sovereign':

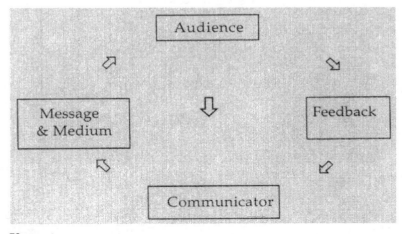

In response to Engel's assertion that the 'audience is sovereign', evangelical Christians immediately want to retort that the 'word of God is sovereign'. But then we look to Jesus Christ, not only as the *content* of our communication, but also as the *role model* of our communication. The words of Jesus are invariably related to the needs or context of his hearers. Paul's sermons and letters were directly related to the issues facing his audience. What was said would often go far beyond the immediate starting point, as with Christ's encounter with the Samaritan woman or Paul's preaching to the Athenians. But in the beginning of communication, the 'audience is sovereign'. Beginning with 'Audience' and moving clockwise, we will explore each of these four components of Engel's process in this chapter.

The Scottish Audience

Looking at our Scottish audience we can divide it into six vital areas where we need to see the Gospel penetrate our nation.

[i] The Third Generation
We are now ministering to the third generation of people in Scotland with no consistent church involvement or Christian teaching through family, school or church. Ministry among children and young people will require imagination and commitment to be the kind of church that makes sense to them.

[ii]   The Gender Gap
There is still a marked division of one man for every two women in the church. Most boys grow up to assume they will grow out of church. If the last two decades have majored on issues of women's identity and role in society, the next twenty years will be wrestling with major issues of male identity and roles. What kind of church, Gospel and leadership draw men to put first the Kingdom of God? What kind of church, Gospel and leadership touch the modern woman with that same commitment?

[iii]   The Left-Outsiders
There are many people who for a variety reasons feel 'left out' by

the church. Many in our Urban Priority Areas assume that the church is not for them. Many whose lives do not fit the patterns of 'traditional family values' assume their lifestyle will be an obstacle to acceptance. Many spiritual seekers assume the codified faith of our fathers is too dogmatic to accommodate them.

[iv]   The Country Casuals

One of the legacies of the parish system is the large number of people with very nominal associations with the church. There may be positive features of this kind of community kinship, especially in rural areas, but it also represents a group of people who have lost, or never enjoyed, a full commitment to Christ and his church. Touching the tens of thousands of former members is another task that assumes a move from making members to making disciples. Making disciples is a skill that will be essential to the future of the Gospel in Scotland.

[v] The Society Shapers

The opinion formers of society seem to share a common disdain for the church and a cynicism about the Gospel. There are sectors of society that require a sensitive but positive apologetic. Tomorrow's communicators have a task of arguing for a Christian worldview which has been dismissed by many as *passé*.

[vi]   The Grey Area

It is wrongly assumed that because the most church members are older, that the majority of older people are church members. It is estimated that 70% of our senior citizens are not members of any church. Many who lifted their lines[2] in the 1960s are lifting their pensions in the 1990s! In the future we will have an increasing number of older people with an ever-decreasing knowledge of the Gospel. Pastoral evangelism among older people will be a much-needed gift.

Listening to the Feedback

If we follow Engel's process, we need to listen to the feedback that is available from our Scottish audience. We draw on two pieces of recent research and a wider observation about culture shifts in our Western world.

Prospects for Scotland 2000: Census of Church Attendance 1994[3]

On 30 October 1994 a Census of Church Attendance was conducted across Scotland. 4164 churches were contacted (did you know there were so many?) and over 80% responded. On that morning 575,000 people were in church, 14% of the population of Scotland.

As was pointed out by Maxwell Craig of Action for Churches Together in Scotland, that means one person in seven was in church. On that basis the evangelistic task is quite simply for each of us to win six others! Start praying!

Grateful we may be for the 'half-full' diagnosis of the water glass, but we have to take seriously the fact that in 1984 the figures were 660,000 people (17%), and the age profiles show a frightening gap between 10 and 30. What are the challenges we need to face?

♦ *Only 5% of the adult population was in a Church of Scotland congregation on the morning of the Census, and only 17% of the population are members of the Kirk.* The Church of Scotland is now in a minority situation in terms of active commitment by the population. General goodwill to the Kirk is no substitute for personal commitment to Christ. Stop making members! Start making disciples!

♦ *18% of Scottish children under the age of 15 were in church that morning. However, under 8% were in a Church of Scotland congregation.* This highlights the importance of after-school clubs and alternative strategies for children's ministries outwith a Sunday. Children's evangelism requires priority attention.

♦ *We lose one third of our children as they move into their teens and we lose half of our teens as they move into their 20s.* We need to develop worship suitable for adolescents if we are not to keep losing more children. We need to give permission for creative alternative churches for young people and others in a given area. Youth ministries need to be released that create new churches rather than simply try to re-enter churches that do not want the hassle of change.

♦   *The most alarming statistic was the fact that only 7% of churchgoers are in their 20s.* This has huge implications for the values that will shape family life in the next generation, and for the leadership of the church in the next 20 years. Who will give quality time to these transitional twenties?

♦   *The '30-somethings' was the only age group showing growth in the last ten years.* Is this bulge in the figures the last remnant of the church-going generation, or the sign that people are marrying and entering the family stage in their 30s rather than their 20s? Or both? Family ministry to this age group will be a priority to 'strengthen that which remains'. The focus must be on supporting them to be the church active in the world, rather than expecting them to enter the cluttered world of church activity

♦   *There is a marked drop in attendance among the over 70s (29%).* Older congregations do not mean that the older generation has been won for Christ. There is much to be done here where memories still carry the treasure of Gospel teaching, but the enigmas of life have suffocated a Cross-less churchianity. The Spirit can still light the living flame of faith.

♦   *There was a marked increase in the number of congregations of under 100 worshippers.* Congregations over 100 need to nurture a sense of purpose and belonging, and to 'close the back door' to lapsing. Perhaps we need to be more positive about the benefits of small churches. Multiplication of small churches may be a better strategy than cobbling together larger units which drift down to the usual manageable level of 25-30% involvement, whatever the size. Belonging and purpose are the key ingredients.

Understanding the Times: **Barriers to Belief** [4]
In 1993 the General Assembly of the Church of Scotland invited *'Presbyteries to assess possible barriers to belief and the general climate of opinion regarding the Christian faith in their areas....'* Presbyteries adopted a great variety of approaches, therefore there was no common method for statistical analysis. However, the responses received from 33 out of 46 Presbyteries were collated and published in 1995 as *Understanding the Times,* identifying four main categories of barrier to belief in Scotland today

♦ *Barriers Relating to Lack of Felt Need*
Many people simply do not know the basic story of Jesus. Others do not care, while others simply do not see any need for God or the church in their lives.

♦ *Barriers Relating to the Secular Climate*
Much is made of the Enlightenment legacy of intellectual trends over 200 years, placing reason and human freedom at the centre of things. There has been a steady marginalisation of religion with 'little shelf space in the supermarket'. Relativism means truth is based on feelings rather than any concept of objective truth. The Gospel may be true for you, but not for me. Materialism prevails over the spiritual dimension of life. The media, education and the secularisation of Sunday were recurring factors seen to be affecting this climate.

And yet, in the midst of this seemingly relentless secularisation, we find a candle of hope quoted from another source: *'Allegedly secular people are far more religious than for many generations.... It is almost avant-garde to be engaged in the spiritual search"* [5]

♦ *Barriers relating to the Intellectual Issues*
There are no surprises here. *Suffering* is a global issue for the young and a personal issue for the older age groups. How often have we heard it said, 'In 70 years and more I have seen no evidence of divine intervention.' *Science* appears to have disproved things Christians believe. Science and belief are thought to be incompatible. Any claims to *specialness* are resisted. There is a reaction to 'special pleading' for Christianity or Jesus Christ in a pluralistic world.

◆ *Barriers relating to the Church*

'Disenchantment with the church came out as a major barrier identified by our survey. This may have been so because interviewers asked questions principally about the church....'[6]

Sometimes it was the church's representatives who were charged with hypocrisy or offering a confused picture of the Gospel. Sometimes people threw the worst elements of our history in our face. Sometimes it was the services that were described as boring, irrelevant, dogmatic, or out of touch, with little opportunity for feedback: 'The Church consists of groups, none of which I feel I fit into. ... If people cannot easily find ways to belong, they will probably not find it easy to believe.' [7]

The report concludes that: 'There are many who are not against the church or belief in God or Christ. They have many questions and there is a lot of misunderstanding of what the Bible teaches or what it really means to be a believer.... We need to get out there to where people are, and be ready to consider where they are at, not where we think they should be.' [8]

The Gospel and Tomorrow's Culture: Culture Shifts

And so we are back to James Engel's call to listen to the audience! One other point of analysis is important to signal here. It comes from the work of Graham Cray of Ridley Hall, in which he highlights major culture shifts in our time:[9]

From	To
Monologue	Interaction
Cerebral	Visual
Development	Ecology
Consumerism	Simplicity
Explanation	Experience
Status	Service
Activism	Mysticism
Linear Thinking	'Bit' Thinking
Believing	Belonging
Argument	Story

It takes only a glance at the left-hand column to recognise the culture of the church. A second thought reveals how the church is captive to a passing culture. One side is not better than the other, but if we do not begin to connect with the right-hand column our Gospel communication will be shouting into the wind.

The Communicator: A Church for our Times

And what about the communicator in Scotland today? In the words of Lesslie Newbigin, 'The best hermeneutic of the Gospel is a congregation that believes it.'[10] 'But one factor was common to all: it was the presence of a believing, worshipping, celebrating congregation of people deeply involved in the ordinary life of the neighbourhood. ... This was no humanly devised programme for mission. It was the work of the Spirit, present in the life of the congregation, flowing out into the community, through faithful words and deeds of members.'

All round Scotland we need Christ-centred communities of faith where people can meet with God. These communities will live *in* the grace of God and live *out* the grace of God.

Living in the Grace of God

The famous hymn about Christ which Paul inserts into his letter to the Philippians (2:5-11) shows us the pattern of grace: how Christ who was rich in glory took the downward journey into our humanity and into death on the Cross, and then took the upward journey through resurrection into glory, reunited with the Father. Karl Barth has defined sin as our refusal to obey the downward call of humility and service, and our refusal to believe the upward call to authority and confidence. It is this double movement that marks a church that lives *in* the grace of God.

On the one hand, the church in Scotland has to choose between death or death: the quiet death of old age or the decisive death of laying down her life in service in order to rise again in the next generation. If a new generation in a new culture is to be touched by the Gospel, then there are many deaths that we have to die shaking us out of our comfort zones of place, language, and style.

The grace of God will not leave us in the place where we are untouchable.

On the other hand, a tired and depressed church needs to believe that we are indeed risen with Christ and the God of resurrection is at work among us. There has been a crisis of confidence in the Gospel, and a failure to rest on the fact that Truth is the person of Christ, ever-living and revealing himself in our times.

Living out the Grace of God

Raymond Fung,[11] former Evangelism Secretary for the World Council of Churches speaks of the 'double dynamic' of a missionary congregation reflecting the nature of God as revealed in the parables of Luke 15 — *going to find* like the shepherd and the woman,[12] and *waiting to welcome* like the father aching for the return of his son.[13] In these two pictures we see the marks of the congregation that is living *out* the grace of God.

Going to find involves being a travelling church — literally going to where people are geographically, culturally, intellectually, emotionally and spiritually. *Waiting to welcome* makes us examine how hospitable we are, how easy it is for people who may be 'not like us' to fit in, and whether broken people sense the warm embrace of the Father or the cold shoulder of the elder brother![14]

Unless the body language of our congregations speaks of the grace of God, the Gospel of grace will remain hollow religious words to the people of Scotland.

A Key Missionary Question

There is a question that will not go away as we face Scotland today. It may be a key missionary question for us amidst the great transitions of our times: *What kind of church will make sense of the Gospel to the next generation?* According to those who vote with their feet, it will not be like the one we have at the moment!

The Message: Good News for our Times

As we move round Engel's process of communication, we arrive at the point where many of us would have preferred to begin: the message and the medium. The message is the same as it was when Peter first opened his mouth on the day of Pentecost, the message about *"this Jesus"*.

He spoke of Jesus, the man of Nazareth, Jesus crucified, Jesus risen, Jesus ascended, Jesus the Spirit-giver and Jesus the life-changer. That announcement spoke directly into the experience of that crowd, within the worldview of the crowd and responded to the questions of the crowd. Perhaps we need to preach that same central message, but with an eye and an ear to our Scottish audience today.

Themes for Today

If Peter were preaching that sermon today, here are some of the connections he might make with his audience.

♦ *Jesus, Man of Nazareth*

What does it mean to be human today in the great "morality debate"?

What is God really like amidst the supermarket of options?

Is God really in touch with our pain and distress?

♦ *Jesus, Crucified*

In a society where "people do not matter any more", we matter to God *this much.*

In a society living by the master myth of progress, the cross exposes sin and evil.

In a society racked by broken relationships, here is forgiveness and reconciliation.

♦ *Jesus, Risen*

The despair of meaninglessness is all pervasive.

The resurrection offers hope both cosmic and personal.

The sense of anxiety amidst so much change is disorientating.

The Emmaus Road speaks of Jesus as a travelling companion amidst change.

♦ *Jesus, Ascended*

People sense that the world is out of control, or manipulated by unseen hands, whether economic or demonic. We speak of the Lord of history and Lord of the chaos, the one who was prepared to be out of control on the cross is now in control of all things.

♦ *Jesus, Spirit-giver*

Ours is an age where spirituality is a buzz word. We can help people follow through that search to a personal relationship with Father. We can be interpreters of the journey for the seekers in company with the Spirit who leads us into all truth.

♦ *Jesus, Life-Changer*

Here is the necessity and the possibility of spiritual change through repentance and renewal by the Holy Spirit. The one goes to the roots of our nature's resistance. The other plants seeds of our nature's renewal.

Amidst the vast changes of our culture there is no reason for us to lose confidence in our message. Drawing on the work of John Leith's *The Reformed Imperative,* [15] we might set our message in the context of our culture using the following schema:

1. Amidst a world of mystery God has made himself known in Christ.
2. Amidst a world of brokenness God offers the way of forgiveness in the cross.
3. Amidst a world of death and evil God brings the hope of resurrection victory.
4. Amidst a world of confusion God's grace is in and through all things for good.
5. Amidst a world of depersonalisation God offers us eternal value by creation and choice.
6. Amidst a world of hopelessness God speaks of a new heaven and earth.
7. Amidst a world of methodology God offers the life and presence of his Holy Spirit.

Models for our Times

However, if we can have confidence in our message, we need courage to adapt our methods of communication – and in some cases abandon them!

♦ *Alpha Courses*[16]

The popular Alpha courses offer a course on Christian basics, but it is presented in a way that combines faith, friendship, food and freshness. The courses offer people an opportunity to discuss, question, pray and travel a journey of faith together. Judging by the hundreds of thousands who are now sharing in Alpha courses across the world, it is an idea whose time has come.

♦ *Creative Arts*

In our visual culture many people are rediscovering the power of the creative arts in opening people up to the Gospel: music of all kinds for all tastes, participative drama in a former video shop, dancing Christmas carols in University, story-telling in the local pub, puppetry at family parties, Christian clowning and mime in streets and congregations. There are numerous attempts to redescribe worship and witness for our culture.

For some of us who have been reared on "words only" this can be very threatening, alienating and disabling. To be part of a creative arts event can make us feel marginalised. Then we realise that this is how many others feel in the settings which we create for ourselves.

Increasingly our society is a non-reading culture. It has been suggested that while the churches are declining in numbers, it may be that we are reaching a fair proportion of the literate population. Unfortunately there is a kind of "natural selection" going on long before people reach our church doors because our communication does not touch the new culture.

♦ *Back to the Bible*

Those of us who believe in the Bible, need to return to the Bible for our models. This book was once an oral tradition of stories, a parade of festivals, a cycle of songs, and a series of conversations with Jesus throwing out mind-bending questions and puzzles. The letters which we read in small sections were written to real people in real places. They were intended to be read aloud to an assembled gathering, not dissected with anatomical skill by the preacher's scalpel.

The Enlightenment mindset of analysis has shaped our communication and will continue to serve the needs of some for time to come. However, there are other Biblical models of communication to be explored if we are to touch our culture in the Spirit of Christ.

The Last Word

In his book, *21st Century Church*, Rob Warner issues a challenge:

'We have nothing against those who as part of their Christian devotion serve Christ according to the patterns of traditional Western culture. These are truly God's people.... But our hearts yearn for the 90% in the modern world who simply will not traditionalise in order to become Christian.... New initiatives in cross-cultural mission are essential, if we have any real intention of reaching the modern world with the unchanging Gospel of Christ.'[17]

That challenge must be faced if we are to communicate the Gospel in Scotland today.

Notes

1. James F Engel, *Getting Your Message Across* (OMF Literature Inc., Manila, Philippines, 1989), p.18.
2. The Church of Scotland Transference Certificate of membership from one congregation to another is colloquially called 'lines'.
3. Peter Brierley & Fergus Macdonald, *Prospects for Scotland 2000* (National Bible Society for Scotland & Christian Research, Glasgow, 1995).
4. Church of Scotland Board of National Mission, *Understanding the Times* (St Andrew Press, Edinburgh, 1995).

5. John Drane, *Evangelism for a New Age* (Marshall Pickering, London, 1994), p.183.
6. *Understanding the Times,* p.38.
7. *Ibid* p.29.
8. *Ibid,* p.34
9. Adapted and schematised by Ray Simpson of Lindisfarne from Graham Cray, *The Gospel and Tomorrow's Culture* (Church Pastoral Aid Society, Warwick, 1995).
10. I have not been able to trace the exact source of these words of Lesslie Newbigin, but they may have been in an article on missionary congregations in the *Expository Times* in the late 1980s. In *Mission in Christ's Way* (WCC Publications, Geneva,1987), p.20, Newbigin expands on the idea when he alludes to a survey of 40 new converts in one industrial area of Madras, and comments:
11. Raymond Fung, *Mission in Christ's Way,* WCC Strachan Lectures presented at the Seminario Biblico Latinamericano, San Jose, Costa Rica in August 1988, Lecture 1, pp.5f.
12. Luke 15:1-10.
13. Luke 15:20ff.
14. Luke 15:20ff, 25ff.
15. Adapted and schematised by me from the key themes in John H. Leith, *The Reformed Imperative: What the Church has to Say that No one Else Can Say* (Westminster Press, Louisville, Kentucky, 1983).
16. *Alpha Courses* have been the basic Christian teaching courses in Holy Trinity, Brompton, London, since the early 1980s. In the 1990s the Rev Nicky Gumbel, one of the staff team, developed and marketed the courses in books, tapes and videos so that hundreds of thousands of people across the world have become involved with them. They have provided the means of spiritual renewal for many Christians and an avenue to faith in Jesus Christ for thousands of people. Published by HTB Publications, Holy Trinity Brompton, London SW7 1JA. First published 1993.
17. Rob Warner, *21st Century Church* (Hodder & Stoughton, London, 1993), p.61.

Chapter 5

A Case Study on Death or Glory

Albert Bogle

A general backdrop

'Death or Glory' is an interesting title for a conference dealing with mission. However, as we approach the third millenium, a better title might well be 'Glory through Death'. The 20th century has become the age of mindless mass violence, ranging from two great world wars to the unthinkable, destructive power of nuclear weapons. Since the 1950s the face of the world has changed dramatically. The church herself has become a victim of what writers like Edith Wyschogrod calls 'the death event'.[1] For her, the whole twentieth-century experience is summed up in that one phrase. At the core of this kind of postmodern thinking lies the belief that since there is no longer any valid 'big story', the world is now in discontinuity. The past age known as 'modernity' has been superseded. Technological advances have ushered in a new, disconnected era where knowledge about things is less certain. To ask the question, What is truth? is to ask the wrong kind of question. Some see in this age of uncertainty an opportunity for the church to be taken seriously in a debate which argues that one point of view is as valid as the next.

In chapter 3, Will Storrar concludes that the Church of Scotland, while having a success story in the 1940s and early 1950s, was unable to adapt quickly enough to a society which was rapidly becoming postmodern. He suggests that the present-day church is still trying to adapt to this loss of status, brought about by the so called 'death event'. He sees the present church going through a mourning experience. Storrar challenges the church to realise that its very nature must call it back to resurrection.

It is this hope and certainty of resurrection that has challenged me to believe that an apparently dead church can come to life and renew a whole community. Therefore, I have spent the last 15 years of my ministry seeking to nurture the signs of life that the Holy Spirit has brought about in our congregation. This is the main thesis of the case study at Bo'ness.

A personal backdrop

'The Church of the 1960s and 70s simply reflected the same decline that was seen in other major institutions in our land' – Jeremy Paxman seeks to substantiate this claim in his book entitled *Friends in High Places*.[2] It was not only the Church of Scotland that was experiencing difficulty with her image. Some denominations seemed even more ridiculous; what about an English Episcopal Church, in the heart of Glasgow, in the midst of an SNP revival? The name alone had the effect of frightening off any potential Scottish worshippers.

I well remember living through this period of change. I was the son of an immigrant Irish family living in Glasgow. We attended faithfully the equivalent of the Church of Ireland in Glasgow, namely St. Silas. It was so alien from all I was experiencing as a teenager in the sixties. While the Beatles were singing *She Loves You, Yeah! Yeah! Yeah!*, we sang English chants to the psalms and repeated prayers in a language that belonged to the museum. The services were conducted in Elizabethan language out of the 1662 Book of Common Order. It was this experience more than anything else that convinced me the church had to change.[3]

Yesterday's problems are still with us

In reality this kind of church service would have to die before another could be resurrected. It has taken the church almost 25 years to bring about modest change. Meanwhile, the world has not stood still but has moved on at an even greater pace. While bands like Ultra Sonic sing rave, and the Spice Girls top the charts with songs like *Two Become One*, the church sings songs that seem as distant from this generation as the English chants seemed to mine. The problem is that the church seems unable to integrate youth culture into worship. When it has tried, it has failed. The Sheffield experiment with the 'Nine O'Clock Service', written about by Roland Howard·, will not go away. Much of the failure he attributes to lack of responsible oversight by those in authority, over those who had been given authority. However, those who had authority claimed they could not understand youth culture. We need to encourage theologians to engage with youth culture, and see ways in which we can legitimately express the gospel in and through it, without compromising the Biblical message.

The question is, was the Church of Scotland recognising Will Storrar's thesis in the 70s? Unfortunately the answer is no. In a decade, where commentators were seeing and recognising these changes, the Church of Scotland produced a hymn book that was wildly out of date even before it was published. It was a book that had taken almost 10 years to compile and reach agreement on. Indeed, some of the hymns, according to John Bell, (a past Convener of the Panel of Worship) have never been sung by a congregation. The church, as an institution finds it very hard to change. Unfortunately, the present revision of the hymnal may fall foul to the same criticism by a generation that has been raised on techno-dance and rave music.

Main-line denominations, like the Church of Scotland and the Church of England, will need to learn to adapt more quickly if they are to survive. I have no doubt that the church will survive, but the form and style or worship may be quite different. We need to look through death to glory.

It was against this background that I found myself the minister of St. Andrew's, Bo'ness in September 1981. The Presbytery arrived and duly ordained me. I was given the keys to the church and expected to get on with things. The city teenager had grown up to become a 30-year-old minister in the Church of Scotland in a small town situated less than an hour from Glasgow and about half-an-hour from Edinburgh on the banks of the Forth looking over to Culross, the birthplace of Glasgow's patron Saint Mungo.

Revolution or reformation

St. Andrew's, Bo'ness, was viewed by the establishment as a good solid kirk for a first charge. This was reflected in its stonework, its giving and its people. It was a congregation that boasted having two past Moderators of the General Assembly as their ministers in the heady days of the 1950s. On my arrival, I received a letter from a prominent churchman at the Church of Scotland's central offices in Edinburgh, congratulating me on being elected to the charge with the inference that it was a good stepping stone to greater things.

However, in the early 1980s the Kirk Session were aware that numbers were falling and that the congregation was aging and in years to come they might not survive. The vacancy committee accepted that change in leadership styles was essential.

A revolution began in 1981; the reformation still continues today. The old church approach had to die in order that the new church could be resurrected. Death has to come before glory. What I am about to describe is not meant to be a blueprint for perfection. There is much that still has to be done and is done despite all of us who are in leadership. We have not got all the answers but we are convinced about the direction in which we are travelling.

Mission is the lifeblood of the church

At the centre of our pilgrimage is our belief that Jesus Christ is the only Saviour of the world and that the Bible is the only reliable instruction book, or map, with which to make the journey. Today the church faces new problems that are related to growth and development. All ages have to be considered, with the arrival of young families, teenagers and young people in their twenties and thirties, as well as those who have been on the journey for a longer period. The leadership had to be continually aware of the changing circumstances of the parish and those who attend worship. This calls for a constant review of all we are doing and of all we have done in the past. One thing is for certain: we are convinced that mission is the lifeblood of the church, and prayer is the oxygen we breathe if we are to stay alive.

Choice could be a key to growth

Worship today at St. Andrew's, Bo'ness is very different from what it was fifteen years ago. In many ways it has come to reflect the needs of the parish and community we seek to serve. There is a choice for worshippers allowing all ages to worship honestly and meaningfully. There is a strong emphasis on music and the visual arts. Banners have become an accepted expression of praise and worship, as all kinds of people share in their making, especially during the lead up to the major festivals in the Christian calendar. Yet it still has a long way to go. Teens and twenties need to be represented more. Later on in the paper I will describe some of our attempts to impact this generation.

You can't stand still

For ten years we laboured with the problem of managing change in order to keep the morning congregation united and happy. Most of the time we achieved this but at the expense of the children.

The teaching facilities were cramped and the experience of some twenty toddlers crammed in a small room while another sixty children of various ages sought refuge in the bigger hall only encouraged at least a 25% drop off by the time Christmas came around each year. Going to Sunday School was not a pleasant experience. Indeed some children opted for the discomfort of a sermon, which had been prepared for adults, rather than attend Sunday School.

It was the postponement of a £120,000 building programme, due to the discovery of a large outbreak of dry rot in the sanctuary, that led us to seek an alternative course of action. This involved a complete new strategy. We took a hard look at worship and started a brand new service at 9.45am. The format would be different without the constraints of a past tradition. We started to use teaching material that was integrated for all ages. Thus adults and children would worship together but learn in their respective age groups. Adults learned together as one group, but looking at the themes the children were being taught. I resisted the temptation to have a 'family service', believing it limited the teaching input that adults received. Instead we opted for all age worship and integrated teaching. The format is as follows:

The 9.45am format

The first fifteen minutes consists of praise, prayer and setting the scene and is followed by the teaching time. Children and adults separate into different areas of the church for their teaching time. The two large transept areas have had all their pews removed and now act as two large open plan teaching areas. These areas are also used at various times during the week by a variety of groups. Pews have also been removed from the front of the church to allow a more spacious chancel area, making room for the praise band and other presentations. Around seventy substantial chairs now replace the front pews.

Adults at the 9.45am service move to the back of the church for an interactive teaching time. After a twenty minute presentation of the theme for the day, a radio microphone is passed around so that the congregation can interact with the content of the teaching time. Questions are often asked, and indeed points added to what has already been given in the teaching time. I believe this is an opportunity for the whole body of Christ to share in ministry. It is a point in the service which allows others who may have a teaching gift to begin to practice their gift in a natural way without them even being aware of what they are doing.

At around 10.30am the Gathering Time song is played and children and adults return together for the final quarter of the service. At this time children and adults share in a newstime relating the stories of their lives during the past week and inviting Godís blessing on their families and friends. This gives the prayers of intercession a different meaning. The topics prayed about have come literally from the congregation there and then. Over the years all sorts of wonderful answers to prayers have been shared at this point.

The advantages of these changes has been that we have established another congregation in the life of St. Andrew's Parish. Many people have said to me, 'But does this not divide the church?'

My answer is that it has united the church, because it has allowed choice, and choice has kept us together. In a missionary sense we have planted a new church which has no preconceived ideas about what church should be like. Yes, it has given us a lot more work, but we have more freedom and space to experiment with contemporary and traditional worship. Many parents are learning the Bible stories for the first time themselves. More fathers are attending worship and seem to enjoy the relaxed atmosphere of the service. Teachers now concentrate on the lesson they are to teach, and the musicians lead the worship songs. On occasions a worship team is formed to plan a series of services.

The flip side
The down side of all this is that the 11.15am service is less busy. In fact it is almost 50% less. This has created a different atmosphere in the church, which some worshippers like and others regret. There is a definite stillness now, for there are no children or flushed parents to be seen. This has made some realise how much they miss the children while others say they can concentrate on worship. Everything has a price tag on it. For the most part the Kirk Session believe the price tag has been worth paying. We have seen a steady increase in those attending the 9.45am service.

At present the 11.15am service is holding its own. During school holidays both congregations come together for joint services. The joint services have proved very important in creating a sense of celebration. Last Easter the church was packed to capacity, although many families were away on holiday. The philosophy behind the split is that we are trying to grow two smaller congregations into two larger ones. The principle is a gardening one. We have thinned ourselves out to allow room for growth. We have planted a new congregation in our building.

My main concern is that we continue to ensure that the two morning services grow and that input continues to be at a high level. Now that the first flush of enthusiasm is over, and a generation of children have experienced church as at the 9.45am service, we need to be continually on the look out for young families to replace those who have grown up and are going off to university, college or work. It is my prayer that we will be able to hold on to those who have come through the 9.45am service but I am aware of the pressures and the attraction of other activities on a Sunday morning. The 9.45am service is a brave experiment which has to been continually worked at.

We recognise that there are now three distinct congregations all working together under the leadership of one Kirk Session. Even worship continues to lead a life of its own 'clientele'. There is little now that will surprise this group of worshippers of all ages. About once every two months we have a healing service, and once each month we have a communion service.

In all of these services I am painfully aware that we are not reaching the vast bulk of the community and especially those who are under twenty-five. We have around 1900 homes in our parish and we have around 400 households in our congregations. What is happening in the other 1500 homes, especially the teenagers?

TGI Sunday

This coming year in 1997 we intend to host a joint service on a Sunday evening sponsored by ourselves and our neighbouring congregation, The Old Kirk. This service will appeal to those who wish to push the boundaries a little further using new technology and traditional liturgies.

Most contemporary Christian worship does not include those who have been influenced by the rave and dance scene. While we need to be aware of the danger of pandering to passing fads and losing traditional imagery because it is not understood by the changing culture, I believe there is a place for experimentation that is still biblically rooted. There is also a place for teaching and explaining biblical imagery and thought-patterns as part of the inherited culture of the church and it is with this in mind that we propose to start a new service on the last Sunday of the month called TGI Sunday (Thank God It's Sunday).

Creative thinking and expression has to take place if we are going to communicate with a generation that is totally sold on music and visual imagery. We need to learn also from the mistakes of those who have attempted to develop this form of worship. The Sheffield experience must not prevent others from attempting to be creative with worship especially in a culture where less than 8% of the youth in our schools share any church connection.

Changing styles of worship in themselves will not bring people back to church. It is the personal relationships that believers build with non-believers that will eventually being about interest. However, it is the authenticity of personal Christian living that attracts the interest of the non-believer, and that is the work of grace that God does in the hearts of both the believer and the non-believer.

The best for God

It is out of a commitment to become the best worshippers possible that we, as a worshipping community, have been challenged to understand the meaning and purpose of mission.

Much of the thinking about mission today has been done by a church that has an inferiority complex. Too many congregations have retreated to the ghetto of self-pity, echoing the words of Elijah in 1 Kings 19:10b, 'I alone am left and they seek to take my life also.' The words of the apostle Paul have been re-worked into the slogan which says, 'Be in the world, but not of it'; or into a mission strategy that says to the people we are supposed to be evangelizing, 'Keep your distance, you might contaminate us.' We need to be subversive and infiltrate the world with confidence and faith.

The inclusive gospel

There has been a failure to speak of the inclusive nature of the gospel. We need to adopt a more reformed position, or should I say biblical position, one that declares, 'The earth is the Lord's and everything in it.' This position calls us to rejoice in our place in the world to celebrate our humanity, to affirm all that is good and true in the world. In the words of the General Thanksgiving in the 1662 Book of Common Order we read, 'We thank Thee for our creation, preservation and all the blessings of this life.' This understanding of the world calls us to feel at home in God's creation. We need to be reminded that when God created the world, 'He saw that it was good.'

In our preaching and teaching we need to realise that the Bible teaches us that humanity is longing for a lost Eden. Men and women have a longing to know God, despite all we hear about our pluralistic society. I believe that the majority of Scots still have the last vestiges of Christian morality lurking deep within them. Perhaps it is not that the people have left the church, but that the church has left the people. As evangelists we need to have a greater biblical understanding of inclusiveness. We need to discover what it means to live out trinitarian theology in the communities to which we minister.

Remember, many of the parables of Jesus relate to mission. The good Samaritan was good enough although he had been excluded by the religious leaders of his day. We need to become people-centred, as Jesus Christ was. So many Christians have removed themselves physically and socially from non-Christians. The longer we are Christians the fewer non-Christian friends we have.

The opportunity to influence
Christian leaders are often the worst offenders in this area, in that they are too busy to socialise. We need to be a part of the salt in the world. Further, we do not encourage enough partnerships with non-Christian agencies. We are so afraid that our standards might be compromised, rather than believing that we might influence the standards of others. By refusing to develop these links we are missing out on vital opportunities to affect our local communities.

I believe that there are many projects and partnerships that will not compromise our faith as we seek the common good of our communities. Seeking to work out this philosophy of mission in the community has led us to initiate four major projects which involve people who are outside the church but who share our common interest in maximising the good in our community.

♦   *The market place*

All these projects, although initially set up by people in St. Andrew's, now involve many people from various congregations in the town. The first project was the establishment of a shop to sell Christian books, cards and literature. We quickly realised that this was not enough to attract a variety of people into the shop so we have diversified over the years to include all manner of unusual gifts.

This has not been an easy project to keep going. There have been times when financially the project has been on the point of collapse. Yet God has given us people with loyalty and commitment and this Christmas, the eleventh year of the shop trading, will prove to be the most successful, allowing us to put well over £4000 into the Trust which distributes help to various third world projects and home mission initiatives. We have around 20 volunteers who work weekly in the shop, and the helpers have a recognised indirect witness to the public. Many people in our town, who have no connection with the church, are making contact with Christ through our daily witness in the market place at the centre of commerce in our small town.

♦   *The oldest cinema in Scotland*

The second project involves a three-way partnership which involved the formation of a youth trust by the churches in the town, now known as the Without Fear Trust (WFT) – the name reflects out town motto. The other partners are The Scottish Historical Buildings Trust (SHBT) and the Rank Foundation, who at present are funding the youth project to around £150,000.

This project aims to work with two kinds of young people – the vulnerable and the less vulnerable. Recently this project has had to reassess its priorities. This has been painful and has involved a temporary setback. However, we have now moved to new premises in the town and we hope to see the project flourish in the new year.

Out of the success of this youth initiative we hope to attract funding which will allow us to develop the oldest cinema in

Scotland. This cinema, in the middle of the town, is now owned by the Scottish Historical Buildings Trust. They in turn have entered into an agreement with the WFT that they will refurbish the building for our use as an Arts Centre. This will involve the SHBT raising just under 1million pounds. The WFT will be responsible for the ongoing expenses of the building and the day to day management of the project.

In this project we hope to see the return of the cinema and the performing arts in the town, as well as a recording facility. At the centre of this project is a vision for the complete economic renewal of the town. This is a vision which we in the church cannot bring about by ourselves, but we can inspire, encourage and help to facilitate the vision. The church in this project is seeking to be the salt and the light in the community.

♦ *Care in the community*

The third project comes out of a desire to serve some of the needs of the community. Dementia is a growing problem. After much prayer and reflection and planning with the Social Work Department, the local Heath Care Clinic and Alzheimerís Scotland, we opened a Day Care Centre for Dementia sufferers, which has now been operational for nearly two and a half years. During this time we have served around 30 to 40 families.

The centre takes nine people in at a time and is staffed with an equal number of volunteers each week. Around 20 people in the congregation participate in this project. It is our wish to welcome all who come to the centre in the name of Christ and offer them the very best care. To date we have a waiting list. This year the Church invested £4000 towards the up-grading of the accommodation on offer. We received many gifts in kind from companies who helped us create a new Church lounge and modern toilet facilities.

This project was initially brought to the Kirk Session by an elder who felt God was calling her to set the project up. The Kirk Session backed her all the way and today the project is going from strength to strength. However, the Kirk Session keeps a close interest in the work and the management committee are responsible to the Session for their work.

♦ Church in the pub

The fourth project is a weekly outreach in the local hotel. Each Wednesday we run a very successful Alpha Course in the hotel, allowing those who never normally come to church to come along and share in the fellowship of discovering faith together with others. During the past three years over 50 people have joined the church through this outreach and a number of lapsed members have been restored.

We try to run at least two Alpha Courses each year; if time permits we try for a third. Alpha is an opportunity to find out about Christianity over a period of three months. During this time friendships are formed and many enquirers find faith. The success of this project, I believe, is not only due to the content but also to the fact that it is a regular weekly commitment that takes place in a neutral venue. There is nothing new about the course. It is a basic enquirers course into Christianity asking questions like, 'Who is Jesus', 'Why did He die', and 'How can I be sure about my faith?'

In these four projects there is an underlying philosophy of inclusiveness. It is a simple one that says, 'Include people until they exclude themselves.' This is surely the Gospel: 'For God so loved the world that He gave His only begotten Son, that whosoever believes on Him should not perish but have eternal life.'

Today, those of us who minister in parish churches have a wonderful opportunity to share the gospel. I believe there are many doors waiting to be pushed open and others that are wide open inviting us to share. Evangelists need to recover that sense of community that made Chalmers work at the Gallowgate experiment, or James Barr identify with the Boiler Makers' Union on Clydeside. The words of Jesus ring out into the third millenium, 'The fields are white unto harvest.' Let us go and discover our calling and enjoy the creative work of the gospel.

Notes

1. Edith Wyschogrod, *Spirit in Ashes. Hegel, Heidegger and Man-made Mass Death* (Yale, University Press, Newhaven,Conn. & London, 1985).
2. Jeremy Paxman, *Friends in High Places* (Penguin, London, 1991*)*.
3. I acknowledge that St Silas Church has undergone immense changes during the past few years and would pay tribute to the present rector, David Richards.
4. Cited in Charles Handy, *The Empty Raincoat* (Hutchison, London, 1994).

Chapter 6

The Church's Mission in Scotland:
A Para-Church Perspective

John Mackinnon

The context for the industry of the people of Israel in Nehemiah chapter 3 is the word of God and prayer. As we read through the chapter it is easy to become bored with the lists of names and the itemised areas of responsibility that were assigned to various individuals and groups. But close examination reveals an all-member-ministry, a body of people working to a well-thought-out strategy and plan. Beginning at the sheep gate the people work in harmony in an anti-clockwise direction, committed to their own field of labour which is essential to the whole enterprise of rebuilding the walls.

It is also refreshing to notice the number of young leaders who are involved in this service of God and who perhaps for the first time are taking on responsibility in the community – a picture which ought to be apparent in the local church and is all to often conspicuous by its absence.

When conducting public worship, I like to read this chapter from a modern translation but with this difference: I read out names not from the book of Nehemiah but the names of those who are members and adherents of the fellowship where I am preaching. The contrast between the original in Nehemiah which the congregation are following in their Bibles and the adaptation I am reading to them with their names substituted for those in the biblical text makes for a pointed and striking exposition of the passage.

Will Storrar has said that parachurch organisations have had their day, and that we need to get back to the local church; (see

Chapter 3 for a fuller discussion of Storrar's views). Now as the Scottish evangelist for Scripture Union there is a sense in which I understand and follow his logic. In response, I have to say that if the church, recognising the biblical rôle of the evangelist, was to employ them among its many other ministries, then I would be happy to consider leaving a para-church appointment and going mainstream. But it must be said that at present there aren't a lot of vacancies for evangelists in the local church. However, I am encouraged at the way Scripture Union as a para-church organisation is seeking to address the issue of the church's mission in Scotland's changing society.

Definition

It is important that the foundation upon which we build is clear, therefore prior to building a case for the continuing ministry in evangelism in which Scripture Union is engaged, let me clarify what I mean by the use of the phrase 'para-church'. David Cohen accurately defines it as follows: 'A para-church organisation literally is one which exists alongside the church, making its resources and skills available so that the church can fulfil its God-given task of communicating the good news to its contemporary generation.[1]

His description of our work as one which is Church-serving is a more accurate way of defining what our ministry is all about. The expression para-church as commonly used and understood creates ideas and notions which are unhelpful, whereas reference to organisations like our own as church-serving agencies adequately illuminates the possibilities our work presents. It's a substantial claim and, like the work in Nehemiah, it demands an integrity that in all our structures, strategies and programmes we should be available to serve the church and to provide for her needs.

A 'jurassic church'

The earlier chapters in this book have warned us against the entrenchment that our churches have fallen into in the past, the dangers of a 'jurassic church' type of mentality where dinosaurs rule and control the church. If we interpret what God is saying in the present, then we need to be culturally relevant in every age. This involves a process of constantly reviewing what we are doing and why we are doing it that way so that we are able to maintain a relevance in the midst of the fast-changing society in which we live.

I believe it is easier to do this from outside the local church than to do it from within. This is why Scripture Union Scotland has spent considerable time redefining its structures and strategies in recent days. The framework produced through these prayerful deliberations has highlighted at least five significant areas in the life of the church's mission. I want to flesh out a little of our activity as a para-church organisation by explaining briefly each of these five areas.

The Role of the Evangelist
The brochure advertising my own work expresses its central conviction in these words: 'Mission is at its best when it ceases to become a sporadic endeavour and becomes the lifeblood of the local church.' This is a calculated and serious attempt to remove the 'hit and run' criticism with which some styles of evangelism have been labelled. It is also intended as an honest commitment to be there for the long haul together.

The pattern of the work has as its primary aim an agreement between the evangelist and a local church or group of churches first to keep on working together for a period of two years and secondly to develop a strategy for evangelism appropriate to the culture of the area. It is an attempt to recreate something of the Pauline principle demonstrated in his work at Ephesus.

The first part of this agreement incorporates a review of all that the church is doing within its community. The aim is to measure the effectiveness of the church's community and outreach work and also to ascertain whether some approaches have passed their 'sell-by date', need fresh resourcing or require a more innovative programme to achieve their ultimate goal.

This element of the evangelist's work is what I sometimes refer to as the Scapegoat Ministry. The majority of church leaders and ministers could identify some (though not all) of the issues that this kind of review produces, but for these leaders to go on to present such issues to the congregation could have the effect of isolating them from their people and producing an impasse.

When however an evangelist brings these findings to the congregation there is often some resentment but it is directed against the evangelist, leaving the leaders and congregation open to work through the matters raised with a degree of harmony. The initial upset at the evangelist is usually short-lived and the opportunity to assess priorities and develop a strategy for more effective evangelism emerges.

The evangelist can then work with the church to create effective programmes in line with the culture of the local church and community. The whole approach aims to address the cultural irrelevance highlighted by several contributors to this book, to facilitate transition and to help the church to become what she should be in mission.

I should add that the role of the evangelist within the movement does still allow for the more traditional one-off mission, normally in the context of Christian Focus Weeks (see below) in schools. In practice, these are often the catalysts for more extended agreements of the type we have just considered.

Christian Focus Weeks and Regional Field Staff

One of the most fruitful ministries among young people in recent years has been the work carried out by Scripture Union regional field staff and evangelists in what we term Christian Focus Weeks in schools. This involves our working closely with the local churches by offering key people as resources to participate in Religious, Moral and Social Education classes during a particular week of the school session.

These resource people would include Scripture Union staff, approved volunteers, chaplains, ministers, professional drama groups and youth workers, all of whom would be considered to be good communicators and who have some training in school work.

During a Focus Week we would work closely with the Christian young people in the school and organise key lunchtime events, incorporating debate, drama, music and discussion. We also work with the local churches to prepare young people's events in the evening where the challenge of the Christian gospel can be clearly presented and the local church can follow up the work that takes place.

The work is supported by the local churches through prayer, finance and their members' involvement. The nurture of any new disciples is committed to the local churches but ongoing future support in personnel and relevant materials is generally offered and would be seen as part of the Christian Focus Week ministry.

Church Based Holiday Clubs

Historically, Scripture Union is associated with the summer months, seaside towns, activities on the beach for children and 'sausage sizzles' for the whole family as a fitting conclusion to a great holiday. Romantic memories are still occasionally expressed today but the present realities of foreign holidays, broken homes and the vast exodus of children from our churches call for a freshness of approach.

The idea of a beach mission in Barbados has a lot of appeal in the snow of a Scottish January but its practical value to the church is negligible. Therefore, the Holiday Activities Department of Scripture Union (Scotland) has developed from the traditional beach mission concept an more contemporary, exciting programme of church-based Holiday Clubs, where local church members are involved as the core team .

Employing the strategic opportunity that school holidays provide we encourage the local church to set aside a week when the building is transformed into an imaginative venue for a club which children thoroughly enjoy and where they can discover the truth of the Bible for themselves. The programme for the week will include lively music, games, quizzes, story-telling, crafts, discovery sheets and drama. While the children will be part of a big group they will also belong to a small group where they can be discipled by a committed Christian small group leader.

As an organisation we seek to provide leadership for these clubs where the church is short on resources but the priority is to develop the gifts and skills of local church people in effectively communicating their faith.

The possibilities and potential of this approach are endless because it is birthed in the local community, targeting specific local audiences and the ongoing relationship is there after the club finishes. I have witnessed thriving midweek children's clubs, whole family conversions and innovative revisions of Sunday Schools as fruits of this partnership approach. The whole emphasis is on local people meeting local people and sharing faith in the Lord Jesus – using an agency like Scripture Union to facilitate the work.

Training

If part of the answer to addressing the church's mission in Scotland is to enable the rank and file membership to exercise fully their own spiritual gifts and put them into practice, then resourcing becomes a major issue. Scripture Union has been responding to the training needs of local churches for many years. More recently, the demand has been so large that the full time staff and voluntary training advisors have been developing a programme for the churches entitled 'Suit Yourself'.

This lets churches and groups opt into training at a time and place which suit, and use the experience of Scripture Union staff and volunteers. It is a subscription-based training where churches buy the number of places that they require and go to courses selected from a menu, much of which is concerned with the effectiveness of the local church in mission. Courses are on both a residential and single day basis.

The provision of such a facility maximises the training potential as well as securing the best trainers in particular fields. It would be difficult, not to say time consuming and expensive, for local churches to arrange similar provision right through the calendar year. But Scripture Union is able to do this, and so serve the local church in this way.

Line Management of Shared Workers
In an attempt to increase the effectiveness of the church's mission among young people many local churches have pooled resources to employ an area youth worker. The idea is admirable, economically effective and in terms of the biblical unity of believers commendable. But there can be problems as to the expectations of church members, as the 'pound of flesh' mentality can make unrealistic demands upon the worker.

Scripture Union (Scotland) has been seeking to develop the value of local area workers and at the same time protect these shared workers in their situation. The agreement is that as an organisation. through our regional staff, we line-manage the local area worker on behalf of the churches. The worker attends Scripture Union staff training and development days, enjoys the fellowship of a larger team and gains access to the vast resources the movement brings to the local church situation. They are also protected from unrealistic work programmes and the end result should be a full-time Christian worker making an impact on behalf of the local churches in their immediate area.

Certain members of the church form the local management committee and retain a hands-on involvement in the whole arrangement but have as a resource the ready ear of a whole youth movement.

Get up and get on
Finally a parable.[2] A group of priests went to a monastery for a weekend retreat. There were Dominicans, Benedictines, Franciscans and Jesuits. As they participated in an evening liturgical service of prayers and chants the lights went out and the entire monastery was plunged into pitch darkness.

Unperturbed, the Dominicans continued with the liturgy which they knew off by heart. The Benedictines, uncertain of the liturgy, fell on their knees and prayed that the light might be restored. The

Franciscans launched into a theological debate about the relative virtues of light and darkness. What of the Jesuits? Well, they got up, went out and fixed the fuse!

To see ourselves as others see us! Is it not time to get up and get on with tackling the massive task of evangelism which faces the churches of today? In facing the challenges, please remember our definition of a para-church organisation: 'A para-church organisation literally is one which exists alongside the church, making its resources and skills available so that the church can fulfil its God-given task of communicating the good news to its contemporary generation.'

Notes

1. Cohen & Gaukroger, *How to close your church in a decade*(Scripture Union, London, 1992), p. 30.

2. Adapted from Cohen & Gaukroger, op. cit. p.66.

Chapter 7

The Church as God's Agent in Mission[1]

Chris Wright

Introduction :Mission and Ecclesiology for Paul

The success of Paul's mission among the gentiles or nations raised the urgent question: 'How can gentile nations be part of the people of God, if membership of that people is defined by circumcision, the Mosaic covenant, and keeping the law?' Paul was forced to justify his mission strategy from the Scriptures (i.e., the Old Testament), and his answer fundamentally was, 'consider Abraham!' (Gal.3:6-8,14,26-29; cf. Rom.4:16-17). From the beginning, Paul argued, it had been God's purpose to bring the nations into the sphere of blessing as part of his people. That was 'the gospel in advance' announced to Abraham. Therefore, the gentile mission was a *fulfilment,* not a contradiction, of the Scriptures. The Abrahamic covenant is the fount and origin of biblical mission in its redemptive sense. For Paul, then, the very nature of the church was defined by the mission of the people of God as announced in the Hebrew Scriptures. So, for us, our ecclesiology must be founded in missiology.

I. THE MANIFESTO OF MISSION

God's people for the nations

The canonical context of the Abrahamic covenant is the engagement of God with the world of nations in the primal history, especially the post-flood table of nations (Gen. 10), and Babel (Gen. 11). So the call of Abram in Genesis 12 is God's response to the problem of the nations of humanity. Indeed, through its use of the terminology of fruitfulness and blessing it echoes the language of creation, indicating that the election of Israel in Abraham is God's means of restoring the creation itself. Here begins the story of redemption that occupies the rest of the Bible until in the final picture we see God and the nations reconciled in the new creation (Rev. 21:1-3, 24-26; 22:2).

The historical content of the promise, as it related to Israel particularly, included posterity, covenant blessing, and land. These elements unfold as the Pentateuch progresses: the nation emerges after various threats; the covenant relationship is established; the boundary of the land is eventually reached (and crossed in Joshua). However, the bottom line of the Abrahamic covenant expresses its universal goal: 'in you/through you, all nations of the earth will receive blessing' (Gen. 12:3, cf. 18:18, 22:18; 26:4-5; 28:14; 35:11). The frequent repetition of this dimension of the promise in Genesis alone shows that it is fundamental and pervasive. Israel's identity, role and destiny is to be integrally linked to God's purpose for the rest of humanity. At least three missiological implications may be mentioned.

A. A universal purpose
There was a universal purpose in God's election of Abraham and of the people of Israel. They were called and brought into existence only because of God's missionary purpose for the blessing of the nations. Indeed, God's commitment to Israel is predicated on his commitment to humanity as a whole. The universality of the Bible's mission to the nations is not a New Testament 'extra', but integral from the very beginning of God's historical action. Echoes of this theme can be found, e.g. in Psalms 22:27; 72:17; Jeremiah 4:1-2 (and see below). Inasmuch as the church's identity is in organic continuity with Old Testament Israel (as Paul insisted in Gal. 3:26-29; Eph. 2:11-3:6), the same universality attaches to it. We exist for the sake of the nations and as the vehicle of God's commitment to them.

B. A unique particularity
The universal goal (blessing for all nations) would be achieved by a particular historical means: 'through you...' The uniqueness of Israel (which is connected to the uniqueness of Yahweh and

the uniqueness of Christ) is a key Old Testament affirmation.
Echoes of this are to be found, for example, in Deuteronomy
4:32ff., Amos 9:2 and Psalm 147:19-20. It is very important to
hold together in balance both biblical (Old Testament and New
Testament) truths: the inclusive, universal goal (God's
commitment to bless the nations); the exclusive, particular means
by which God chose to do so (Israel, and through Israel, the gospel
of Christ).

C. A missionary people
God's commitment is to bless the nations through a particular
people. Thus, *the primary agent of mission is the people of God.*
God's answer to the human predicament was not to whisk off
individuals to heaven, but to create a new community on earth
who would be a 'light to the nations'. Jesus' command to his
disciples, 'You are my witnesses' (Luke 24:48; Acts 1:8) was an
echo of Yahweh's word to Israel, similarly entrusted with the task
of confirming to the nations the identity of Yahweh as the true
God and source of salvation (Isa. 43:10-12). Mission is not merely
a task for missionaries, but the *raison d'etre* of the whole people
of God. Our ecclesiology must be founded in missiology, and
vice-versa! – as it was for Paul.

Thus, our first affirmation is:
*The Church is God's agent of mission – by its very existence
and calling.*

II. THE SIGN OF MISSION

God's people among the nations
If we define mission solely in terms of being sent from one place
to another with a message, then there is no mission at a national
level in that sense in the Old Testament (although Jonah would fit
the description, and the other prophets certainly were sent with a
message, even if they did not cross national boundaries).

Mission, however, has the wider meaning of a purpose, a task.
For Israel as the people of God that purpose and task were *to be*
something rather than *to go* anywhere. Israel was to manifest a

distinctive identity and life among the nations. They were, in a sense, to be a sign pointing to the true God, or in the precise phrase of Yahweh in Isaiah 43:12, 'You are my witnesses,' declares the LORD, 'that I am God.' We shall sample just three texts that express different dimensions of this identity and role: Deuteronomy 4:32-40; Genesis 18:19; Exodus 19: 3-6.

A. Covenantal uniqueness: Deuteronomy 4:32-40

This summarizing section at the climax of a very significant chapter emphasises first *Israel's unique experience* of revelation (at Mt. Sinai), and of redemption (through the exodus) in verses 32-34 and 36-38. The implication of the rhetorical questions is that no other nation in human history had experienced what Yahweh had done for Israel. This is not to say that Yahweh was not interested or involved in the history of other peoples; Deuteronomy has affirmed as much already (Deut. 2:9-12, 18-23) But Israel's experience of historical revelation and redemption was unprecedented and unparalleled.

This produces, therefore, secondly, *Israel's unique knowledge and witness* (v. 35). The purpose of the unique experience was 'so that *you* might know...' the truth about the identity and nature of God. What other nations do not as yet know, Israel knows, because Yahweh had proved it in their history. The same dynamic is found in Isaiah 40–55, where the 'missionary' implications are more forcefully drawn. The knowledge of the living God was something entrusted to Israel as part of what it meant to be a 'light for the nations'.

That knowledge, thirdly, was of *Israel's unique God* (vv. 35-39). Old Testament monotheism was not merely a matter of arithmetic (only one God exists), but of the defining of the personal and redemptive character of God: 'YAHWEH is God... and there is no other'. This has important implications for the distinctiveness of biblical monotheism and of the New Testament Christology which is integrated into it (e.g. 1 Cor. 8: 4-6).

The church, then, is God's agent for mission because, like Israel, we have been entrusted with a unique experience of redemption and a unique revelation of the knowledge of the living God.

B. Ethical distinctiveness : Genesis 18:19

The ethical challenge of Deuteronomy 4 is already visible in verse 40, and is given missional flavour in the Deuteronomic theology of, for example, 1 Kings 8:60f., but other texts illustrate more forcefully the ethical challenge that was part of Israel's mission in the purpose of God for the nations. The combination of ethics and mission can be found as early as the programmatic patriarchal narratives, and especially in this key statement in Genesis 18:19:

> For I have chosen him so that he will direct his children and his household after him to keep the way of the LORD by doing what is right and just, so that the LORD will bring about for Abraham what he has promised him.

This little divine soliloquy comes in the middle of a narrative that includes Genesis 18 and 19, the story of God's judgement on Sodom and Gomorrah. It significantly nests this reminder of God's universal promise of blessing in the midst of a story of God's historical judgement. This in itself helps us address the problem often raised as to how the Old Testament can talk about God's purpose to bless the nations when the nations are frequently the target of wrath and judgement (notoriously here, and later in the conquest narratives). The eschatological expectation for God's ultimate intention of bringing blessing to the nations of humanity did not nullify the moral sovereignty of God over the behaviour of specific nations in the course of history. God could use the Israelites as agents of his moral iudgement on the Canaanites, just as he would later use a whole catalogue of successive nations and empires as agents of his judgement on Israel itself. Yet his long term goal remained steadfast: through Israel the nations would ultimately find blessing.[3]

We see, first, Sodom, as a model of our world. Sodom represents the way of the fallen world of human wickedness. Its evil is prototypical and proverbial. We hear of the 'outcry' (se'aqah) that betrays oppression and cruelty (Gen. 18:20-21); of the perverted and violent immorality of the inhabitants (Gen.19); of the comparison with the bloodshed, corruption and injustice of Jerusalem (Isa. 1:9ff.); and of the arrogance, affluence, and callousness to the needy that makes it sound very modern (Ezek. 16:49).

Secondly, we meet *Abraham, a model of God's mission*. In the context of impending judgement, God 'recaps' his purpose in verse 18. God's promise of a son in the first part of the chapter is now seen in the light of this expression of his mission goal in the second part, and in contrast to the world to which he is on his way 'down'. God, on the way to act in judgement on a particular evil society, stops to remind himself of his ultimate purpose of blessing to all nations, and has a meal with this old couple, still childless, in whom the whole divine plan of redemption is invested. Not surprisingly they find it wryly amusing.

But thirdly, we hear of 'the way of the Lord', *as a model for God's people*. The central phrases of verse 19 indicate God's more immediate thinking. In the context of a world going the way of Sodom, God wanted a community characterized by the 'way of the Lord'. This rich Old Testament expression describes not only God's own characteristic behaviour, but also our imitation of him (cf. Deut. 10:12ff.). It is further defined by that pair of words that virtually summarizes Old Testament ethics, 'doing righteousness and justice'. This, says God to God's self, is the purpose of having chosen Abraham, and the means to fulfilling his promise to him of blessing the nations. Thus the syntax and logic of Genesis 18:19 bind together in a single sentence: election ('I have chosen him'); ethics ('way of the Lord... righteousness and justice'); and mission ('what he has promised' i.e., 'all nations on earth will be blessed'). The ethical quality of life of the people of God is the vital link between their calling and their mission. There is no mission without ethics.

C. Priestly holiness: Exodus 19:3-6

After the exodus, we are with Israel at Mount Sinai. Exodus 19:3-6 is a key, a programmatic statement by God, coming, like a hinge in the book of Exodus, in between the exodus (Ex. 1-18), and the covenant and law (Ex. 20-24). It defines the identity and agenda God has for Israel and sets both in the context of God's own action and intention.

The divine speech points, first, to *God's redemptive initiative* (v. 4). 'You have seen what I have done... ' God's initiative of saving grace was a matter of historical fact and recent memory. We need to recognize the priority of grace in Old Testament theology of mission and ethics. Obedience to the law was based on, and was a response to, God's salvation (and definitely not a means of earning or obtaining it). Exodus has 18 chapters of redemption before a single chapter of law. As the agent of mission, the church is responding to the grace of redemption.

Secondly, we hear again of *God's universal interest* (v. 5b): 'Out of all nations...' 'The whole earth is mine...' God's very special place for Israel (his 'treasured possession'), their identity and task, is here set in the context of his universality as God in relation to the nations of the earth (cf. the similar balance of particularity and universality in the Abraham covenant). Therefore, the ethical and missional agenda for Israel has to be motivated by the same universal concern that characterizes Yahweh as God. Interestingly, Peter's use of this text in relation to the identity and role of Christians likewise emphasizes our living 'among the nations' (unfortunately NIV translates as 'pagans' 1 Pet. 2:12).

This leads, thirdly, to *Israel's identity and duty* (v.6).

(1) A priestly kingdom

To understand what this means for Israel as a whole in relation to the nations, we have to understand what the priests were in Israel in relation to the rest of the people. They had a twofold task: (i) *Teaching the law* (Lev. 10:11; Deut. 33:10; Jer. 18:18; Mal. 2:6f.; Hos. 4:1-9). Through the priests, God would be known to the people. (ii) *Handling the sacrifices* (Lev. 1–7 etc.) Through the priest's work of atonement, the people could come to God. The priesthood was thus a two-directional representational task between God and the rest of the Israelites.

It is thus richly significant that God confers on Israel as a whole people the role of being his priesthood in the midst of the nations. As the people of Yahweh they would have the historical task of bringing the knowledge of God to the nations, and bringing the nations to the means of atonement with God. In this way they would also fulfil another function of the priesthood which was (iii) *conferring God's blessing on the people*. Just as Israel's priests blessed them (Num. 6:22-27), so Israel would bless the nations. This dual movement is reflected in prophetic visions of the law/ light/justice etc. of Yahweh going out to the nations from Israel/ Zion, and of the nations coming to Yahweh/Israel/Zion. The metaphor easily connects with the centrifugal and centripetal dimensions of Old Testament eschatology. The priesthood of the people of God is thus a missionary function.

In the New Testament Peter sees the priestly nature of the church as 'declaring the praises' of our exodus God ('out of darkness into light"), and living in such a way among the nations that they come to glorify God (1 Pet. 2: 9-12).

Significantly also, in the only New Testament text to speak of any individual Christian's ministry in priestly terms, Paul describes his evangelistic mission to the gentiles as his 'priestly duty' (Rom. 15:16). Sadly the church forgot that priesthood is what happens outside the walls of the church in mission to the world and imported it back into the internal ministry of the church, where the New Testament never refers to it.

(2) A holy nation

For Israel to fulfil their mission of being Yahweh's priesthood in the midst of the nations, they must be 'holy'. The word was not exclusively, or even primarily 'religious' (in our sense, at least), but fundamentally meant, 'different, distinctive'. Israel was to be a nation among the nations, but to be recognizably, visibly and substantively different, as the people belonging uniquely to Yahweh and therefore representing his character and ways to the nations who did not yet know him as God. Holiness is both a fact (it is something God does to or for us, cf., Lev. 20:8; 26:21:8, 15, 23; 22:32), and a command (it is something we work out in life, cf. Lev. 18:3; 19:1; 20:7, 23, 26) . For Israel, the command, 'You must be holy because the Lord your God is holy', basically meant: 'You must be a different kind of nation, because Yahweh is a different kind of God.'

Leviticus 19, prefaced by that command (v.2) is a key text,

giving practical down-to-earth content to holiness.

The list of ethical distinctives for God's people include: family and community respect (vv. 3, 32); religious loyalty (vv. 3b, 4-8, 12, 26-31); compassionate economic relationships (vv. 9-10); justice in workers' rights (v.13); social compassion (v.14); judicial integrity (v. 15); neighbourly attitudes and conduct (vv.11, 16-18); distinctiveness (v.19); sexual integrity (vv. 20-22, 29); exclusion of idolatrous and occult (vv. 4, 26-31; racial equality (vv. 33-34); commercial honesty (vv.35-36). The moral challenge of this chapter has lost little of its sharpness, for today's church and world, even when all allowance has been made for cultural and historical transference.

If Israel were to be God's priesthood in the midst of the nations, then they had to be different. This reinforces again the integral relationship between mission and ethics in biblical thinking The chief agent of God's mission to the nations is the people of God. The chief requirement on the people of God is that they should be what they are; live out their identity.

So our second affirmation is:

The church is God's agent of mission: by its distinctiveness in experience of God's redemption and revelation, and in its ethical life among the nations.

III. THE GOAL OF MISSION

God's people to include the nations
The eschatological vision of the Old Testament envisages the nations being brought in to share the blessings of salvation enjoyed by Israel. This, of course, is consistent with the promise inherent in the Abrahamic covenant. 'Israel', in fact, comes to be re-defined and extended in a way that underlies Paul's missionary theology of Jew and Gentile in Christ. The theme of 'the nations' is particularly rich in the Old Testament but only a few aspects relevant to the mission of God's people can be mentioned here.[4]

A. The nations as 'observers' of what God was doing in Israel
God's actions in and through his people were on an open stage,

intentionally. Like the light on a lampstand or the city set on a hill in Jesus' comparison, there was to be a visibility to the nations, who would ask questions and draw conclusions, whether positive or negative (cf. Ex. 15:14-16; 32:11f.; Deut. 4: 6-8; 29:22-28; Ezek. 36:16-23).

B. The nations as 'beneficiaries' of Israel's salvation-history

Israel's worship had an astonishing 'faith-imagination' in relation to the nations, who would somehow be the beneficiaries of what God had done in Israel, and could therefore be called upon to celebrate it even though it paradoxically includes the defeat of some nations by Israel in the conquest.

There are many examples of this invitation to the nations to join the praise of Yahweh (e.g., Pss. 47:1-4; 22:27-28; 67; 96:1-3; 98:1-3, etc.) How it could happen was, as Paul put it, a 'mystery'. Even the Deuteronomic history perceives the universal 'missionary' significance of the temple in Jerusalem (1 Kings 8:41-43, 60f.).

C. The nations ultimately included, along with Israel, as the extended people of God

The Old Testament amazingly envisages the full inclusion of nations along with Israel. They would no longer be applauding observers, but would be absorbed into an extended Israel (cf. Ps. 47:9). Some of the prophetic texts that envisage this are quite breathtaking in their scope and boldness; for example, in Isaiah, arch-enemies of Israel will be gathered in (19:19-25), also previously excluded categories of people (56:3-8), even some of the ingathered nations would become missionaries (66:18-21)! Amos 9:11-12 is quoted in the New Testament to provide scriptural legitimacy for the gentile mission of the early church (see Acts 15:16-18).

This great vision lies behind Paul's understanding of the multinational nature of the eschatological community created in the Messiah, as the fulfilment of the mission of Israel. Hence he saw that the very essence of the Gospel was its power to break down barriers and create a 'new humanity' in which there was neither Jew nor gentile (cf. Eph.2:11–3:6; Rom.9–11).

Our third affirmation, then, is:

The church is God's agent of mission: by its inclusiveness as the demonstration of the living power of the gospel.

IV . THE NATURE OF MISSION

God's people as servants for the nations

A significant part of the vision expressed in the last section was expressed through the concept of The Servant of the Lord. In Isaiah 40–55, this term is used for Israel, as the servant people of God, intended to be his witness among the nations, but failing because of their sin and God's judgement. It is then apparently applied to a coming individual who will fulfil the mission of Israel, and explicitly take the justice, compassion, light and liberation of God to the nations (Isa. 42:1-7; 49:1-6).

A. Jesus' sense of mission

Primarily, Jesus saw himself as sent to restore Israel (cf. John the Baptist), in line with Old Testament (and intertestamental) hopes, and particularly in line with the mission of the servant (Mark 10:45, etc.) But the vision of the ingathering of the nations is there, though not fulfilled in his earthly ministry, except in some symbolic words and acts (Matt. 8:5-13; 28:18-20; Luke 24:45-48; Acts 1:8).

B. Paul: Apostle to the Nations ('Gentiles')

In Acts 13:44-48, Paul applied the Servant texts (Isa. 49:6) to himself and clearly understood it as authentication of the Christian mission to the nations. In Romans 15:8-12, Paul sees the servant-hood of Christ to the Jews as the means of fulfilling the promise to Abraham, i.e. blessing to the nations (hence the quotes from the Old Testament referring to the nations rejoicing with Israel). Clearly the New Testament sees Jesus as The Servant, but the servant nature of the people of God is found again in the mission of the church.

So our fourth affirmation is:

The church is God's agent of mission: by sacrificial service in the world.

V. THE COMMUNITY OF MISSION

God's people as disciplers of the nations

Finally, then, to the Great Commission itself – where some may have expected to begin! – Matthew 28:16-20. Far from being an appendix to the Gospel, these verses are the climax and key to the whole Gospel, in which its major themes are gathered up and applied to the ongoing mission of the apostles.[5]

Note especially Matthew's view of mission as discipling. This points to a definite continuity between what Jesus has done for his disciples and what he now commands them to do *for the nations*. This discipling includes both 'baptizing' and 'teaching'. The Church is thus perceived as a community of learning and living by the will of God. The instruction 'teaching them to observe all that I have commanded you...' is pure Deuteronomy! Mission involves creating out of the nations communities of obedience as God had wanted Israel to be. Here again we find a strong continuity between Old Testament and New Testament in the mission and ethics of God's people.

And so we come to our fifth affirmation:

The church is God's agent of mission: by living as a community of discipleship, and replicating such communities among the nations.

Select Bibliography

D. Burnett, *The Healing of the Nations: The Biblical Basis of the Mission of God* (Paternoster, Carlisle, revised edition, 1996).

R. Hedlund, *The Mission of the Church in the World* (Baker, Grand Rapids, Michigan, 1991).

K. Gnanakan, *Kingdom Concerns* (IVP, Leicester, 1993).

D. Bosch, *Transforming Mission* (Orbis, Maryknoll, NY, 1991).

P. T. O'Brien, *Gospel and Mission in the Writings of Paul* (Paternoster, Carlisle, 1995).

C. Wright, *Knowing Jesus through the Old Testament* (Marshall Pickering, London, 1992).

Notes

1. This lecture was based on some of the material that I teach at All Nations Christian College in a course entitled *The Biblical Basis of Mission.* Some of it has also appeared in an article, 'The Old Testament and Christian Mission', *Evangel* 14.2, Summer 1996, pp. 37-43.

2. This is a theological affirmation that I have explained further in my book *Thinking Clearly about the Uniqueness of Jesus* (Monarch, Crowborough, 1997), pp. 89-105; and c.f. also, idem, *Knowing Jesus through the Old Testament* (Marshall Pickering, London, 1992).

3. I have discussed this theological and missiological tension further in *Deuteronomy, New International Biblical Commentary* (Paternoster, Carlisle, 1996), pp. 108 -115.

4. Cf. C. H. H. Scobie, 'Israel and the Nations: An Essay in Biblical Theology', *Tyndale Bulletin* 43.2 (November 1992), pp. 283-305. See also *Knowing Jesus through the Old Testament,* pp. 44-54.

5. For an excellent discussion of the mission theology of Matthew's Gospel, see D. Bosch, *Transforming Mission* (Orbis, Maryknoll, NY, 1991), pp. 56-83.

Chapter 8

Revival and Mission

David J. B. Anderson

In approaching this weighty and significant subject, I am reminded of the story of the educational psychologist who was convinced and taught wherever he went that in bringing up a family, love was the all important thing and so corporal punishment was wrong in all circumstances. One day, the good man was in the process of completing a new path in his front garden. The cement was still wet, the pattern was set when all of a sudden his 12 year old rushed through the front gate. Too late he realised, poor lad! His feet were truly embedded in the path. Whereupon the little lad was cuffed over the ear by his angry father and sent packing and crying into the house.

At that point, an inquisitive neighbour peered over the hedge and said rather provocatively, 'Well Mr Downie, I always thought you were the one who taught that corporal punishment is wrong and love is everything, but I hae ma doots after that!' To which the psychologist very honestly replied, 'That's the problem. I love him in the abstract, but not in the concrete!'

It seems to me that whatever our particular interest in the subject of revival, this is not a matter simply for polite debate or academic discussion but one for clear biblical thinking allied to concrete action. Many are the students of revival and I count myself as one of them, though a very modest one. But how we need theologians, ministers, church leaders, ordinary Christians, not just to believe in the reality of biblical revival, but to pray and to live each day with holy expectation of all that God desires and God promises to his people in these days.

So with that practical desire to address not just the head but the heart – 'theology on fire' – I wish to address myself to certain key questions of historic as well as contemporary significance.

First, why is revival important? Second, what is revival? I want to us to notice the indicators of true revival. That will involve me in offering a general definition and identifying some key distinctives. Third, what about the human-divine aspect – our part and God's part in revival and mission? We will look at the issues of revival and mission, both theological and historical. Finally, what of the future? Death or glory? – to take the theme of this book. So we shall conclude by looking at some of the practical implications that flow from a biblical view of revival and a radical commitment to mission – the implications of revival and mission.

Since the series of lectures on the mission of the church which formed the basis of this book were given to celebrate the 150th anniversary of Evangelical Alliance, you can imagine my delight when I discovered from no less a student of revival than J. Edwin Orr in his ground-breaking study of *'The Second Evangelical Awakening'*, sentences such as these:

> The first outbreak of extraordinary revival in England, the Newcastle-on-Tyne movement in 1859, gave rise to such a happy degree of Christian cooperation that the work was designated 'the Engelical Alliance revival'.... Perhaps the greatest contribution of the Evangelical Alliance to the 1859 revival was its programme of prayer.... Far more than in personalities the Evangelical Alliance influenced the 1859 awakening by its principles. One was its testimony to the unity of all believers in Christ.... There seems no doubt that the whole of the 1859 revival movement was one great unofficial Evangelical Alliance in itself. [1]

But that was 1859! The state of the world and the scene in the church has changed so much that we need to raise again the age-old question of the Psalmist, 'Will you not revive us again, that your people may rejoice in you'![2]

The Importance of Revival

The need of God's people

We turn then to look firstly at the importance of revival. Why is this theme of revival so important now? There is first of all the need of God's people. Revival is of the greatest significance for practical reasons. It is self-evident that the state of the church is far from healthy – 'Facts are chiels that winna ding,' as Robert Burns put it. The facts are that, according to the recent church census,[3] we are in Scotland losing the equivalent of one congregation 225 strong each week, 3% fewer people are attending church regularly (17%-14% of population in the past 10 years) and there has been a large haemorrhaging of young people from the church, especially in the 10-19 age range. Without discounting several very positive indicators, and I happen to be more optimistic in my interpretation of the census than many others, the truth of the matter is the church is losing ground, losing grip upon the people of Scotland and is in 'maintenance mode' largely rather than 'mission mode'. We are digging in for survival rather than praying for revival.

Even a cursory glance at the history of God's people in the Old Testament would make us aware of something that has been true in our own history and especially at times of revival. Stated simply, there is it seems to me a direct correlation between the health of God's people and the state of the nation. In times of reformation and renewal the Church has been wonderfully used of God to influence the moral and spiritual temperature in the nation. Equally, as we see only too clearly today, a decline in Christian conviction and church commitment over the years leads all too easily to a *laissez faire* morality, a pick-and-mix idolatry, a basic godlessness with all its dreadful consequences in terms of social breakdown and human lawlessness.

That is the *status quo* that so many appear to uphold and support, but as Will Hutton, editor of the Observer commented recently, 'The *status quo* is just a euphemism for the mess we are in!'[4] The facts make for uncomfortable reading. The church sows the wind, the nation is reaping the whirlwind.

As historians of revival have pointed out, the twentieth century was the first century since the reformation when there has not been spiritual awakening on a nationwide scale. A fresh outpouring of the Spirit of God upon the people of God – nothing less than this is needed, if we are to begin to reverse the tide of spiritual and moral decline in the church and across the nation. This is the need of God's people. This is why revival is so important today.

The nature of God's purposes

Secondly, there is another reason more compelling still. Revival is also significant because of the nature of God's purposes. Not just for practical reasons but for theological reasons. Few of us here I suppose would dispute that Jonathan Edwards, the 18th century American preacher and writer, is the classic theologian on the subject of revival. During his ministry at Northampton, Massachusetts, a local revival broke out in 1734 and 1735 and a wider awakening across the whole of New England and beyond from 1740-42. He wrote various books and pamphlets on the subject, the most familiar of which are, *A Faithful Narrative of the Surprising Work of God* (1737),[5] *The Distinguishing Marks of a Work of the Spirit of God* (1741)[6] and *An Humble Attempt to promote Explicit Agreement and visible Union of God's People in Extraordinary Prayer for the Revival of Religion and the Advancement of Christ's Kingdom on Earth* (1747).[7]

The last of these is a particularly significant work based on what was happening in Scotland at that time. In the providence of God that model of prayer is being used again as a paradigm across the United Kingdom and Ireland, Europe and many other countries of the world by literally thousands of prayer groups in preparation for revival in coming days. All these works, which are just a small part of his prodigious output, I heartily commend.

There is, however, one other work which sadly is less well known but which provides us with probably the best systematic understanding of how Edwards viewed awakenings and revivals as such and in particular the relationship with God's plan for man's salvation. It is his *History of a Work of Redemption.* As I understand it, there are three key stages in Edwards' thinking here and in his other works about the nature of God's purpose for the world.

First the central purpose of the world, according to Edwards, is to reveal the glory of God. He restates the doctrine of the Trinity without diverging from orthodox doctrine, and in a profound and often moving way, expresses the joy of the whole Godhead in communicating love internally to one another and externally to the creation at large.

The glory of God is thus the chief end of all God's works and it is seen supremely in the way he communicates himself to human beings for their happiness and his own delight. According to Edwards, this is the nature of God and the purpose of God for His world. 'God created this world for the shining forth of His excellency and for the flowing forth of His happiness. The great and universal end of God's creating the world was to communicate Himself to intelligent beings.'[8]

The question then arises what is the principal way in which that purpose is accomplished? The answer according to Edwards is to be found in God's amazing work of redemption. 'All God's works of providence in the moral government of the world are subordinate', says Edwards, 'to the great purposes and end of this great work ... whereby men are brought into a new existence and are made new creatures.'[9]

But for this work of redemption to be effective in its workings and extensive within its scope according to Edwards, God has it in his heart from time to time to communicate that glory most wonderfully by a sovereign and spiritual work of redemption which will transform not just a few individuals but whole communities, even nations. So it is clear according to Edwards in his *History of a Work of Redemption* that spiritual awakening is absolutely central to the fulfilment of God's purpose for the whole world. 'From the fall of man to this day wherein we live, the work of redemption in its effect has mainly been carried on by remarkable pourings out of the Spirit of God. Though there be a more constant influence of God's Spirit always in some degree attending His ordinances yet the way in which the greatest things have been done towards carrying on this work always has been by remarkable pourings out of the Spirit at special seasons of mercy.'[10]

In other words, for Edwards the essence of the revival experience always arises from the inner trinitarian life of God. That is his own internal glory and nothing should therefore detract in revival times from the greatness of the Father in his eternal purpose for creation, or the greatness of the Son in his costly purchase of our redemption, or the greatness of the Spirit in his convicting and converting power. Equally, if the essence of the revival experience is trinitarian, the expression of that revival experience is the glory of God transforming human hearts in their multitudes from darkness to light.

Is it not this very thing that the prophet Habakkuk saw as he glimpsed into God's future for his people in one of a number of as yet unfulfilled prophetic statements about the future of the world? 'For the earth will be filled with the knowledge of the glory of the Lord as the waters cover the sea.'[11] Not a promise about another world, but as many of the Puritans in particular insisted, a real promise for this world, albeit for a time yet to come.

This is the glory of God in the work of redemption by means of the outpouring of the Spirit. This is the nature of God's purpose for our world today in these last days until Christ returns. And who is to say knowing the greatness of our God and knowing what is happening even now across our world that God will not do what God has promised he will do in time to come?

The necessity of God's power

Thirdly, revival is important for biblical reasons because of the necessity of God's power. The most compelling reason for revival is not the state of the world but the need of the church. Only when the need of the church is met locally, nationally and globally will the state of the world be impacted and changed. Unless l am very much mistaken the paramount need of the church today is in Paul's memorable words, 'To know Christ and the power of His resurrection'[12] and in that sense to experience in fullest measure what the early church knew as normative and regular – 'the immeasurable greatness of His power in us who believe'.[13]

This is the biblical mandate for revival: the need of the church; the nature of God's purpose is such as to demand the necessity of

God's power. How can an individual accomplish anything for God without this? 'Apart from me,' said Jesus, 'you can do nothing.'[14] How can a church fulfil its God-given purpose as His agent of mission simply by changing its structures, varying its worship style, communicating in popular user-friendly terminology and engaging in appropriate new forms of evangelism unless it is in Zechariah's timely words, 'Not by might nor by power but by my spirit'?[15] That is why, in the estimation of some scholars such as Andrew Bonar, confirming Jonathan Edwards' earlier observation, we find in the Old Testament alone some fourteen instances of what we might broadly call revival. From Genesis 4:26 when men began to call on the name of the Lord through Exodus, Joshua and Judges (five seasons of revival), Samuel, David and Solomon, the revivals during the reigns of Asa, Jehoshaphat, Hezekiah and Josiah and then after them the remarkable work accomplished under such as Haggai and Zechariah, Ezra and Nehemiah.

Personally, I am not convinced that these instances are all examples of revival. Sometimes they are more times of reformation and covenant renewal. There is also the whole problem of reading back into the Old Testament period examples of that outpouring of the Spirit which was fully realised only at Pentecost.

Yet even a brief survey of the Old Testament evidence apart from the better-known paradigm of Pentecost which Martyn Lloyd-Jones highlights so effectively in his book on revival[16] and of the remarkable times of refreshing following in the history of the early church seem to underline one indisputable fact about the church in this time as in every time. We have the divine mandate 'Go into all the world and preach the gospel'[17] but so often we lack that effusion of life and power to equip the workers, energise the work and evangelise the world. This is why revival is so important. The Bible makes it clear again and again that to fulfil God's purpose we desperately need more of God's power.

Listen to these words of J. Edwin Orr in his conclusion to *The Second Evangelical Awakening*, 'Evangelicals are agreed that the power of God is still the same, that the need of the people is the same, that the remedy is the same in the 20th century as in the first. Only methods and manifestations and men differ from generation to generation. There is much in the Divine Plan as revealed in scripture to suggest that the world but needs a Divine Impulse and a human response. There is nothing in the Divine Plan as revealed in history to forbid that hope.'[18]

The Indicators of True Revival

What is revival?

Having established the great importance of revival for practical, theological and biblical reasons, we need now to take seriously both the biblical and historical evidence to answer the question, 'What is revival?' Misunderstandings and counterfeits abound even today. I remember a woman, a shop assistant, in Gorgie some years ago. As one of our members was chatting to her she commented, 'I know there is a revival going on in that church'. Well it's true, God was at work and the church was growing and we were committed to praying for revival as a believing community on a regular basis. But my view of what she said would be this: if there had been a revival in Gorgie you would have heard about it by now! You don't have to advertise a revival. Like the church in an American town earlier this century which displayed on its notice board for all to see 'Revival here – every night except Monday'.

There is a fundamental misunderstanding here. Unlike mission, revival cannot normally be announced beforehand, organised by the church or promoted by evangelists in a particular time and place. Revival is of God!

Another *caveat* needs to be entered here. God is God and as such he delights in variety and, unlike many a preacher, he does not indulge in endless repetition. So if in reading about the great revivals of the past, biblical and post-biblical, we think we are discovering how God is going to work again, then be prepared to be surprised. Surprised not just because revival is a surprising and sudden work of God, but because when God comes in revival power to a community it is always a new thing that He does. It is true, there are certain common and constant factors recognisable in genuine revival, but why should we ever dare presume God is going to do a new thing in our time which will somehow neatly conform to our categories? One of the things that theologians amongst others can suffer from as they grow old is not, I fear, the hardening of the arteries so much as the hardening of the categories! Is there any limit to what God can do at any one time in any one place? I do not think so.

Consciousness of God

To clear up any misunderstanding then and to clarify what is meant by this word in its biblical and historical sense, what are the indicators of genuine revival? First there is the consciousness of God. In revival, God is seen as God and experienced as God, as when in the temple, Isaiah saw the Lord in all His glory, then saw himself in all his guilt.[19] Or again as at Pentecost when the first believers were all gathered together in one place and suddenly, sovereignly, supernaturally, God breathed from heaven and they were so conscious of Him that all else faded from view.[20]

Speaking out of his experience of revival in Lewis from 1949-53, Duncan Campbell commented, 'The outstanding feature is this deep sense of God, this consciousness of the eternal, men moved with bowed heads. The realisation of God in the midst so overwhelming that sometimes they dare not move.'[21] Arthur Wallis, the Christian writer, underlines the challenge which faces the church in these terms: 'How many today are really prepared to face the stark fact that we have been outmanoeuvred by the strategy of hell trying to meet the enemy on human levels by human strategy. In this we may have succeeded in making people church conscious, mission conscious, even crusade conscious without making them God conscious.'[22] The spirit of revival is the consciousness of God.

Conviction of sin

The second key element in genuine revival is the conviction of sin. If the day of revival reveals the glory, majesty and holiness of God it follows as night follows day that those brought into a new God-consciousness will become deeply aware of their own sinfulness. This can cause weeping and misery. It may produce certain physical effects such as jerking or falling down or similar unusual physical manifestations. But these external effects neither prove nor disprove the reality of revival. The key thing in all such cases as in the three examples in the opening chapters of Acts[23] is that people are internally and deeply impacted by the Spirit of God. When Peter preached the truth about Jesus crucified, risen and exalted on the day of Pentecost under the anointing of the Spirit, Luke tells us of the congregation's response: 'When the people heard this, they were cut to the heart and said to Peter and the other apostles, "What shall we do?"' (Acts 2:37). Significantly, the Greek word for 'cut' here suggests a hammer blow and a violent experience like that of the Psalmist who saw himself and his sins in the light of the mercy of God and cried out from the depths of his need, 'If you, O Lord, kept a record of sins, who could stand? But with you there is forgiveness.'[24]

The fact is, without this deep uncomfortable and humbling conviction of sin we may question whether it is genuine revival. And indeed when revival comes, those who have longed for it most may suffer most conviction in it. Evidently during the revival in Lowestoft when God came in power in 1921 strong fishermen were literally thrown to the floor under conviction. One eye-witness reported, 'The ground around me was like a battlefield with souls crying to God for mercy.' So the consciousness of God leads to the conviction of sin. That brings us to our next point.

The centrality of Christ
The third indicator of genuine revival is the centrality of Christ. As God is revealed and sin is revealed so in times of revival Christ is invariably revealed also as God's sufficient answer to man's sinful agony. Sometimes it is that Christ is revealed prior to that conviction of sin as happened at Pentecost. 'No man can preach himself and Jesus Christ at one and the same time,' commented the great Scottish theologian James Denney.[25] It is true, for Peter preached not himself, simply Jesus, only Jesus. His life attested by miracles, his death attributed to men, his resurrection accredited by God. 'This Jesus whom you crucified, God has made both Lord and Christ.'[26] It was compelling, convicting preaching because it

was in essence Christ-centred preaching: 'This Jesus…'.

Brian Edwards, who recently researched and wrote on this whole subject of revival, *Revival – A People saturated with God,* came to this conclusion: 'All whom God uses in exceptional times of spiritual power, both within the Bible and since then, are men and women who trust the word and place it at the centre of their belief and practice. They test everything by it. In times of spiritual decline, the church will resort to all kinds of antics to gain a crowd and stir enthusiasm. Our response should be to cry to God for such an awakening that will put preaching back in the centre of our worship and evangelism and Christ back at the centre of our sermons.'[27] George Whitefield commenting on the 'Cambuslang Wark' or Revival of 1742 simply commented 'Talk of a precious Saviour and all seemed to breathe after Him.'[28]

The coming of the Spirit

Accompanying such Christ-centredness there is however another fourth indispensable factor in genuine revival – the coming of the Spirit. Why were 3,000 ordinary men and women gathered together in Jerusalem at that time, so conscious of God, so convicted of sin, so convinced about Jesus, that Jesus was for them and for them alone as if they were the only ones for whom he died? Peter tells us right at the beginning of his Pentecost sermon. This is what Joel spoke about. This is the Spirit of God at work. 'In the last days God says I will pour out my Spirit on all people.'[29] This is what happens in revival. Revival is more than a great meeting. It is a meeting with God. More than a great campaign, it is a great coming of the Spirit in which human personalities are eclipsed because God is at work in extraordinary power in his people and through his people on the community at large.

Duncan Campbell speaking at Keswick in 1952 about the revival in Lewis and describing how one after another not just individuals but whole communities fell under the sway of the saving Spirit of God described it thus: 'Under a starlit sky, with the moon gazing down upon us, and angels, I believe, looking over the battlements of glory, were men and women on the road, by the cottage side, behind a peat stack, crying to God for mercy.

Yes the revival had come! For 5 weeks that went on – we had found ourselves in the midst of a God-movement of the Holy Spirit.'[30] Whatever else revival is, it is most definitely this – a God-movement of the Holy Spirit.

Resulting transformation

There is therefore a fifth and final indicator of genuine revival. It is the consequence of transformation. Sometimes secular critics of what are called 'religious revivals' in history dismiss them as religious hysteria or fanaticism. They explain them in terms of the personalities involved and regard them as of no permanent value. Unfortunately we have to admit such comments do contain more than a grain of truth. The fact still remains however that where these four indicators are powerfully present, the consciousness of God, the conviction of sin, the centrality of Christ and the coming of the Spirit, there is inevitably the resulting transformation in the life of individuals, in the life of the church and in the community of society at large.

Take one biblical example, the revival in a city, Samaria, when Philip preached Christ and there was an unusual receptivity to the gospel. [31] Many were touched by God, healed of physical afflictions and delivered from the dominion of evil; there were many conversions, many transformed lives. No different from a successful evangelistic mission. People were changed. That's the bottom line. That's the proof of a real work of God. Yet in another sense so different, not in nature so much as in extent, for the degree and depth of transformation was such as to impact a whole city! 'So there was great joy in that city.'[32]

A careful study in the history of revival will underline the truth that fundamentally the work of mission and the work of revival are not different in nature. The same truths are preached. The same God is at work by his spirit. But if we try to compare the fruits of normal mission and evangelism with the work of revival in a town or a community we see the spiritual, moral and social consequences of transformation are far greater, far deeper, far more widespread and, in the last analysis, they defy totally any merely human explanation.

Let me put it this way. What God does in over 50 years of normal faithful spiritual labour can so quickly and so marvellously be surpassed in just a few days of genuine revival. Mission is about man taking the initiative, in response to God's call, led by the Spirit, preaching Christ, sometimes seeing people come to personal faith, and more rarely seeing conversions in large numbers. Revival by contrast is about God taking the initiative. God coming to a people or place at the appointed time and pouring out His Spirit in such a sense that whole communities, in Duncan Campbell's words, are 'saturated with the presence of God'.

Listen to these words of Jonathan Edwards describing the awakening in Northampton, Massachusetts in 1735: 'There was scarcely a single person in the town, old or young, left unconcerned about the great things of the eternal world. Those who were wont to be the vainest and loosest were now generally subject to great awakenings and the work of conversion was carried on in a most astonishing manner and increased more and more. Souls did, as it were, come by flocks to Jesus Christ'. Edwards then significantly concludes with a remark which describes both the true character and the transforming consequences of this and any genuine revival. 'This work of God as it was carried on and the number of true saints multiplied, soon made a glorious attention on the town so that in the Spring and Summer following, 1735, the town seemed to be so full of the presence of God'.[33]

This is the essential difference between *mission* – the church fulfilling the divine mandate to engage in continuous evangelism and *revival* which, in Arthur Wallis memorable words is, 'Divine intervention in the normal course of spiritual things. It is God revealing himself to man in awful holiness and irresistible power. It is such a manifest working of God that human personalities are overshadowed and human programmes abandoned. It is man retiring into the background because God has taken the field. It is the Lord making bare his holy arm and working in extraordinary power on saint and sinner.'[34]

To my knowledge, there has never yet been a revival which has not been spoken against. In my view, revival provides on an intellectual level as well as an experiential level the unanswerable argument for the reality of God. Even the most hardened sceptics can find themselves compelled to acknowledge the amazing spiritual, moral and social transformation that takes place when God comes to a town or a city in unusual power. Then whether they will admit it or not, they know God is in that place.

Revival and responsibility

There are however at least two crucial issues regarding revival and mission which demand at least a brief airing if only because historically and to the present day they tend to bring confusion rather than clarity. Worse still they can even promote division just at that time when unity is most needed to secure the blessing of God. These issues both concern our part and God's part in revival and mission, the human and divine aspects of a genuine work of God.

If revival is a sovereign work of God what about our human responsibility – revival and responsibility? That is one issue. And the other issue has a long historical pedigree but has recently surfaced in the church because of controversy over the 'Toronto Blessing', and more significantly perhaps as the result of a recent work published by Banner of Truth *Revival and Revivalism..* This second issue concerns the possibility of promoting or 'getting up' revival.

Looking at the whole question of revival and responsibility first, perhaps I can best encapsulate the heart of this problem by referring to news I received some years ago from the church in Malawi. 'The south of Malawi,' the report said, 'is experiencing a very fast growth especially in the city churches. One such congregation regularly adds 500 to its membership each year. The gospel is really touching the lives of ordinary people and the expansion is not superficial. In some churches, the benches, the pulpit steps, the floors are filled each Sunday with many outside unable to get in'. Now if such things were to happen in my church or your church, 500 extra members a year, we would probably call that revival.

But listen further. The report concludes, 'On the human level, this is due to the dedication of many lay people who are prepared to give up weekends, evenings, even meals for the sake of evangelism, pastoral work and Christian care.' We may ask how far was the growth of the church due to the total dedication of these ordinary folk? How far on the other hand do we discern something more here than simply ordinary Christians willing to pay the price to declare with their lips and to demonstrate in their lives the reality of God's love? Only God knows the complete answer to that question.

The simple and perhaps the truest answer we can venture is that they worked as if everything depended on them and God worked because in reality they depended on Him for everything. If I understand revival and mission both biblically and theologically, it is never a question of 'either or' but is always a question of 'both and'. It is a work of God but one that involves human means in which the sovereign power of God and the spiritual preparedness of His people go hand in hand. The word of God stresses again and again these two foundations of every revival.

A classic textual basis for this view is the history of the early church where God's sovereign promise 'you shall receive power' (Acts 1:8) led to the united, believing prayer of the early disciples, which of course resulted in the outpouring of the Spirit at Pentecost. The history of revival, not least the last known revival in this country in Lewis, offers us many examples of the same paradigm. Believing prayer based on the sure promise of God has again and again shaped the future of the church.

Two errors must at all costs be avoided here. The error of *fatalism* involves an extreme view of the sovereignty of God and, if I am not mistaken, is current amongst at least some in the church today. On this view, if God is going to send revival it will come. There is nothing we can do so we need not be especially concerned. Such an attitude ignores the fact that again and again when God has worked in sovereign power he has invariably used human beings and a time of spiritual preparation to that end.

The other view by contrast *over-emphasises the importance of spiritual preparedness* by strongly implying that if we fulfil certain conditions, if we do certain things, we can have revival in the same way we can have electricity. Flick the right switches and God is at our beck and call. This is the problem of what Iain Murray calls 'Revivalism – using human means improperly and unbiblically to promote a work of God.'[35] We shall look at this in a moment.

At this point, it is important to notice how David's momentous words preserve the balance of biblical truth, 'Thy people shall be willing in the day of thy power.'[36] God alone can initiate, determine and inspire by his Spirit the day of his power. That is his *sovereign prerogative*. But on that day it is also true to say his people will be found prepared and willing. That is *our responsibility*. There is something we all must do, something we all can do to believe in and prepare for that momentous day of extraordinary blessing. Believing his promises, our responsibility is fundamentally about our response to his ability. Far from contradicting the fact of his sovereignty, it complements it beautifully and timeously in the outworking of the strange and mysterious purposes of God!

Revivalism
Before we look, however in our closing section at the practical implications that flow from our responsibility, it is vital that we move from this issue of revival and responsibility, and make a brief response to our second issue, the whole area of revival and revivalism. While Murray's book of the same title is largely about American evangelicalism from 1750-1858, the issues it raises are in my view crucial to any right understanding of what constitutes Biblical revival and what, on the other hand, carries too much of human finger prints to be explained in terms of a sovereign work of God.

Murray's thesis is first of all that from 1750 onwards there was, with some few exceptions, a broad consensus amongst evangelicals about the New Testament understanding of revival. For example, Joel Hawes, minister in Connecticut in 1832, would have spoken for many when he said, 'The whole theory of revivals is involved in these two facts; that the Holy Spirit is concerned in every instance of sound conversion and that this influence is granted in more copious measure and in greater power at some times than at others. When these facts concur, there is a revival of religion.'[37]

Second, around the 1820s and more particularly during the time of Charles Finney's remarkable ministry in the middle of the century, this earlier view of revival began to be regarded as limiting if not outmoded. 'Revivalism' as described by Murray and illustrated from extensive historical research, used human means, emphasised human methods and justified human techniques to ensure that the greatest number of people were affected. 'After-meetings' and the 'altar call' were two means increasingly used to exert pressure for a decision.

Third, the consequences of these new methods were to prove disastrous not just in the short-term but in the long-term also. Technique in many instances became more important than truth. According to Bernard Weisberger, in his history of the great revivalists: 'If salvation was for the asking then a revival was getting the greatest possible number to ask as a matter of salesmanship. As theology grew simpler, technique became predominant.'[38]

A further consequence of revivalism was that, in the eyes of many, manipulation by man became more evident than the movement of the Spirit. Seasons of revival took the form of revival meetings. If you took certain steps, certain results were more or less guaranteed. Revival was there almost for the asking. 'Revivals are always spurious when they are got up by man's device and not brought down by the Spirit of God', writes Gardiner Spring, Pastor of the Brush Church, New York, from 1810-1873.[39] The end result, as Murray argues passionately and meticulously, was that revivalism and revival began to be regarded as one and the same thing and because of the human excesses of the former, the latter – the genuine coin – became increasingly discredited.

An issue of crucial importance

This issue of revivalism and revival so helpfully highlighted by Murray is one of tremendous importance in the church today. On the one hand I am not fully convinced that the distinction he makes between revivalism and revival is as easy to make in the heat of the battle as it is on the printed page a hundred years later. At times also, it is possible to discern much greater good being wrought by some of the revivalists for all their faults than Murray gives them credit for. Having said that, even those who do not go all the way with Murray would still agree with his central contention that today perhaps as never before we need to 'recognise the all important distinction between religious excitement, deliberately organised to secure conversions and the phenomenon of authentic spiritual awakening which is the work of the living God.'[40]

Revival and Mission

So far we have seen the great importance of revival and the genuine indicators of revival and we have sought to grapple – albeit all too briefly – with two of the key issues of revival and mission, namely, 'Revival and Responsibility' and 'Revival and Revivalism'. We are now therefore in a position to draw out for the future of the Church some key practical implications which flow from a biblical vision of revival and a radical commitment to mission. I suggest at least three areas demand mature biblical reflection and concrete Christian action.

Firstly there is the whole area of Christian leadership. Here especially in the light of the revival/revivalism issue I believe we cannot stress too much the importance of vigilant participation in the work of God. That will mean not standing on the sidelines because of secondary issues, but increasingly partnering other churches and other groupings committed as we are to gospel work, because we have together the overriding conviction that Scotland will not be won for Christ through isolation and prejudice but only through involvement and partnership! The world will not believe God has sent me, Jesus is saying in his great High Priestly prayer, till you model in Christian love and biblical unity that oneness that I enjoy with the Father (see John 17:20-23). Where this is happening in different parts of Scotland today, I see God is blessing his church in significant ways.

Yet our participation will not be careless of truth. It will call for discernment, vigilance and courage on the part of all those involved, or else what the church most needs and God most desires will once again become tarred with the same revivalist brush as it did in the nineteenth century and as it has done ever since. While a revival that is not spoken against is unlikely to be a genuine revival, some people will invariably look for any excuse to deny a real work of the Spirit. My point is we cannot any longer afford to opt out of partnership with other Christian leaders and churches who are followers of the Lord, whether it be in planning for mission or preparation for revival. However, in opting in, the crying need is for more mature, less manipulative leadership – I mean a leadership which values the gift of discernment, and which seeks to assess what is happening according to proven biblical criteria. Here is the litmus test of biblical validity: 'Do not put out the Spirit's fire; do not treat prophecies with contempt. Test everything. Hold onto the good. Avoid every kind of evil' (1 Thess.5:19-22).

A second area of concern relates to the Christian church as a whole here in Scotland. For those with eyes to see, the need for a vigilant yet whole-hearted participation in mission and revival preparation is all too obvious. Yet, there is still little evidence, especially within our larger denominational and evangelical groups that our churches have taken seriously enough the critical juncture we are at. There is an urgent need for a costly crucifixion at the heart of the life of the church. Are we willing to die to that which has been good in our past, though not indispensable, in order to embrace what is best for God's glory and for the evangelisation of Scotland? Death or Glory? That is the question which lies at the heart of all in this book.

It was 'death or glory' that was so central to the life of the body of Christ in the flesh, crucified as he was to bring glory to God in the conversion of the nations. It is equally central to the progress of the body of Christ in the Spirit through his people if we are to complete the unfinished task of bringing the world to his footstool. William Orchard is right when he says, 'It may take a crucified church to bring a crucified Christ before the eyes of the world.'[41]

I recently came across these words from Derek Baldwin, author and lay reader in the Church of England: 'The church which believes that its life lies in its own heritage and concentrates exclusively on preserving it will find it has nothing left; but the church which realises that its life is in Christ and is prepared to spend everything to make him known to the world will find itself renewed and enriched.'[42] Yes, if the church is to fulfil God's mandate in coming days, vigilant participation must be accompanied by costly crucifixion, personal as well as corporate, as Jesus himself illustrated so clearly both in His life and in His death. 'Truly, truly, I say to you, unless a grain of wheat falls into the earth and dies it remains alone. But if it dies. it bears much fruit' (John 12:24). In this profound and biblical sense, it seems to me death is the real key to the glory of God in the church and in the nation. That brings me appropriately to my final point.

The third area that has significant implications for the outworking of God's purpose in mission and revival is in many ways the most important of all, the area of vision. 'Where there is no revelation the people cast off restraint' (Prov.29:18,NIV; 'Where there is no *vision* the people perish' RSV, AV). If I may say so, that is a biblical analysis of our present condition in the church and nation, post-Dunblane.[43] We desperately need Christian leaders faithful to the word and will of God – Christian leaders of prophetic vision who have heard that still small voice and will communicate God's word for our times without fear or favour whatever the opposition or the cost. 'We do not see our signs; there is no longer any prophet and there is none among us who knows how long.... Have regard for thy covenant, for the dark places of the land are full of the habitations of violence... Arise, O God!' (Ps.74:9,20,22). I believe if the Psalmist were alive to day in Scotland he would be urging us all to plead with God and to pray to God for that very thing. Where is the Lord God of Elijah? In the critical situation we face as a church and as a nation, is there any word from the Lord? In the time of David, God raised up such men for that particular hour of history. 'Of Issachar,' says the Chronicler, there were 'men of understanding of the times to know what Israel should do' (1 Chron.12:32).

It seems to me very significant that in the seven letters to the churches in Revelation 2-3, this is the repeated refrain, the one constant theme, the only common feature in our Lord's words to each of the churches and to the church as a whole. Jesus said, 'He who has an ear let him hear what the Spirit is saying to the churches.' Certainly, as far as mission and revival is concerned, this could be called the day of small things. But more and more wherever I travel I see God at work in a new way. The huge escalation in the number of evangelical ministries in the Church of Scotland and across all the denominations certainly portends something of strategic and future blessing which has no adequate human explanation. There are more and more encouraging signs that God is bringing barriers down and building his church up in readiness for a new dawn.

Yet perhaps most significant of all is the increasing momentum of united, believing prayer across the villages, communities and cities of our land. We see this happening more and more. But we also see it bearing fruit in terms of an increasing number of people, young and old, some of them in rural communities, finding faith in Jesus Christ. Is this mere coincidence? Surely there is something more? Could it be Providence?

Listen to these words of Matthew Henry: 'When God intends great mercy, he sets his people praying.'[44] Now I am no prophet, but everything I hear from God in these days and see across Scotland – far more than there is time here to share – confirms me in the view that God is doing a new thing and preparing us for far greater things at this time. God still loves Scotland and, through many shakings, I believe he is preparing for us a kingdom that cannot be shaken, where ordinary prayer will become extraordinary, where conversions in ones or twos will give way to multitudes in the valley of decision. Up and down the length and breadth of Scotland the winds of the Spirit will blow again as they have blown before, only in greater and fuller measure.

One final word. I believe with all my heart when historians of the final years of the twentieth century and the early years of the new millennium record the events of our time they will point to some of these significant signs of hope in this period of transition and preparation. Furthermore, they will witness to the fact that at such a time as this, though hidden from public view, more and more of the leaders of the church and the people of God were willing as never before to pray with faith, to prepare with perseverance and to pay the price for the land they love and for the Lord they love most of all. On that day, God will come to Scotland through death to glory. There is no other way and I believe it is the way the Master beckons us 'He who has an ear, let him hear what the Spirit is saying to the Churches' (Rev. 2:7).

Notes

1. J. Edwin Orr, *The Second Evangelical Awakening* (Marshall, Morgan & Scott, London, 1949), p217.

2. Psalm 85:6.

3. Peter Brierley and Fergus Macdonald, *Prospects for Scotland 2000: Trends and Tables from the 1994 Scottish Church Census* (Christian Research & National Bible Society, 1995).

4. Will Hutton, *The Observer.*

5. C. C. Goen (ed.), *The Works of Jonathan Edwards, Volume 4, The Great Awakening* (Newhaven & London, 1971).

6. ibid.

7. Stephen J. Stein (ed.), *The Works of Jonathan Edwards, Volume 5, Apocalyptic Writings* (Yale University Press, Newhaven & London, 1977).

8. Harvey G. Townsend, *The Philosophy of Jonathan Edwards from His Private Notebooks* (Westport, 1972), p.130.

9. Paul Ramsay (ed.), *The Works of Jonathan Edwards, Volume 8, Ethical Writings*, (Yale University Press, Newhaven, 1989), p.489.

10. John F. Wilson (ed.), 'History of a Work of Redemption', *The Works of Jonathan Edwards, Volume 9,* (Yale University Press, Newhaven, 1989), p.143.

11. Habakkuk 2:14.

12. Philippians 3:10.

13. Ephesians 1:19.

14. John 15:5.

15. Zechariah 4:6.

16. D. Martyn Lloyd-Jones, *Revival – can we make it happen?* (Marshall Pickering, Basingstoke, Hants, 1986).

17. Matthew 28:18.

18. J. Edwin Orr, op. cit., p.267.

19. Isaiah 6:1ff.

20. Acts 2:1ff.

21. Duncan Campbell, 'The Revival in the Hebrides', *The Keswick Week 1952*, (Simpson, Richmond, London), pp 145f.

22. Arthur Wallis, *In the Day of Thy Power*, (CLC, London, 1956), p.ix.

23. Acts 2:37f; 7:54f; 5:1f.

24. Psalm 130:3f.

25. Found on a plaque in Tain Parish Church with inscription to James Denney, Ross-shire, Scotland.

26. Acts 2:36.

27. Brian Edwards, *Revival—A People Saturated with God*, (Evangelical Press, Darlington, 1990) p.110.

28. Arnold Dallimore, *George Wh itefield*, (Banner of Truth, Edinburgh, 1970), p.128.

29. Acts 2:17.

30. Duncan Campbell, op. cit., p.145.

31. Acts 8:4ff.

32. Acts 8:8.

33. Ola Elizabeth Winslow(ed.), 'A Faithful Narrative of the Surprising Work of God', *Jonathan Edwards Basic Writings* New American Library, New York,1966) p.101.

34. Arthur Wallis, op. cit., p.20.

35. Iain Murray, *Revival and Revivalism*, (Banner of Truth, Edinburgh , 1994).

36. Psalm 110:3 (Authorised Version).

37. Edward A. Lawrence, *The Life of Joel Hawes*, quoted by Iain Murray, op. cit., Introduction, p. xiv.

38. Bernard Weisberger, *They Gathered at the River: The Story of the Great Revivalists* (Little, Brown & Co, Boston, 1958), p.271.

39. Gardiner Spring, *Personal Reminiscences of the Life and Times of Gardiner Spring*, quoted by Iain Murray, op. cit., Introduction, p. xv.

40. Iain Murray, op cit., Introduction, p. xix.

41. William Orchard, *A Treasury of Quotations on Christian Themes* (SPCK, London, 1976).

42. Derek Baldwin, *Dying to Live* (Eagle, Guildford, Surrey, 1995), p. 108.

43. The reference is to the massacre in Dunblane in 1996 of 13 schoolchildren and a teacher.

44. Matthew Henry, Commentaries, Vols 1-6 (Marshall Brothers, Edinburgh & London).

Contributors

Dr David Smith: for many years Principal of Northumbria Bible College; now Assistant Director of the Whitefield Institute, Oxford

Dr David Bebbington: Senior Lecturer in History at the University of Stirling

Dr Will Storrar, Senior Lecturer in Practical Theology, University of Glasgow

The Revd Dr Chris Wright, Principal of All Nations Christian College, Ware, Hertfordshire

The Revd Peter Neilson, formerly Director of the St Ninians Training Centre, Crieff; now Associate Minister of St Cuthbert's Parish Church, Edinburgh

The Revd Andrew Bogle, Minister of St Andrew's Church, Bo'ness, Church of Scotland

John MacKinnon, Field Worker in Evangelism, Scripture Union, Scotland

The Revd David Anderson, General Secretary of the Evangelical Alliance, Scotland and formerly a parish minister with the Church of Scotland